A Skills-Based Approach to Developing a Career

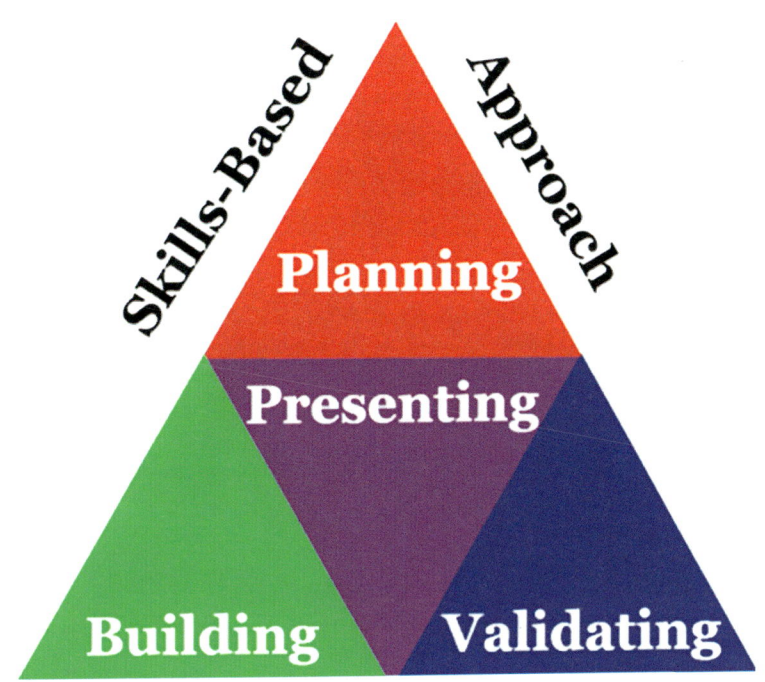

Ryan M. Frischmann

Order this book online at www.trafford.com
or email orders@trafford.com

Most Trafford titles are also available at major online book retailers.

© Copyright 2013 Ryan M. Frischmann.

All rights reserved. No part of this publication may be reproduced, stored in a retrieval system, or transmitted, in any form or by any means, electronic, mechanical, photocopying, recording, or otherwise, without the written prior permission of the author.

Printed in the United States of America.

ISBN: 978-1-4669-8609-1 (sc)
      978-1-4669-8608-4 (e)

Because of the dynamic nature of the Internet, any web addresses or links contained in this book may have changed since publication and may no longer be valid. The views expressed in this work are solely those of the author and do not necessarily reflect the views of the publisher, and the publisher hereby disclaims any responsibility for them.

Our mission is to efficiently provide the world's finest, most comprehensive book publishing service, enabling every author to experience success. To find out how to publish your book, your way, and have it available worldwide, visit us online at www.trafford.com

Any people depicted in stock imagery provided by Thinkstock are models,
and such images are being used for illustrative purposes only.
Certain stock imagery © Thinkstock.

Trafford rev. 07/16/2013

 www.trafford.com

North America & international
toll-free: 1 888 232 4444 (USA & Canada)
phone: 250 383 6864 • fax: 812 355 4082

For the past six years, I have been developing websites, and in the past two years I have been focusing on a personal website service – essentially a platform where professionals can build their own website. I conceptualized a mainstream personal website service in January 2011, and early in the development process, I realized the importance of integrating skill sets into the fabric of a personal website. I saw skill sets as an essential component in making a personal website searchable. This is when I came up with the skills-based approach and I decided to include functionality in a personal website to support each stage of the methodology. I coded the use of skill sets into the personal website interface. This included an internal search mechanism based on skill sets; assigning skills to experiences; and validating skills with certifications, samples of work, and references. In addition, I conducted extensive research to understand how skill sets are currently being utilized by professional web services—such as LinkedIn's social-media platform and Monster's job board. In my opinion, the biggest improvements these companies made to their web services over the past two years are related to using skill sets. Finally, I anonymously surveyed 119 human-resource professionals to understand how they perceived the use of skill sets and if my proposed methodology would be effective. The resonating message from the survey affirmed that most of the respondents are utilizing skill sets to find candidates for employment, and it is possible to plan and develop a career based on them.

I completed coursework toward an MBA from the University of Maryland and earned a degree in management science from SUNY Geneseo. While working toward an MBA, I remember countless afternoons perfecting my résumé and conducting peer reviews with my classmates. This is where I was exposed to the importance of career planning and development. The feedback I got from my peers gave me valuable insights about how others perceive me (and many times it centered on my core competencies). And while reviewing my peers résumés, I appreciated how important it is to plan and develop a career that differentiates my skill set from their skill sets (especially considering we all graduate with the same degree).

One of the reasons I have become passionate about career planning is that most students and young professionals do not spend enough time considering how to best prepare for their future. With the rapid pace of technology and globalization, professionals must plan the development of a skill set—a combination of technical and transferable skills necessary to achieve career aspirations. The best thing to base that career plan on (for example, passions or core competencies) is debatable. Professionals should consider several approaches when they plan their career because there is so much at stake. I think a career is an opportunity, your one chance to make a unique contribution.

To aid the reader, this book is designed as a handbook, with illustrated core concepts and succinct points that will be easy to refer back to. Finally, I avoid using first person and real names, though some of the examples are based on actual stories.

Ryan M. Frischmann

Contents

INTRODUCTION vii
SKILLS-BASED APPROACH 1
Planning Stage 3
    Craftsman's Mindset 4
    Passion Theory 6
    Sometimes the Passion Theory Works 8
    Product to Market 10
    Self-Awareness 12
    Career-Planning Takeaways 13
    Translating Planning Results to Skills 14
    Career-Planning Considerations 16
    Developing an Action Plan 18
Building Stage 20
    Assessments 23
    Setting the Stage 25
    Finding a Mentor 27
    Learning Methodologies 29
    Decisions 30
Presenting Stage 31
Validating Stage 34
    Sample of Work 37
    A Blog 39
    References/Endorsements 40

Conclusions **46**
   Part of Your Personal Online Brand 46
   A Simple Solution 47
   Moving Forward 49
Appendix: Application of Methodology **51**
   Website Developer Career 51
   Salesman Career 56
   Teacher Career 59
Appendix: Transferable skills **61**
   Traditional Transferable Skills 60
   Emerging Transferable Skills 62
   Soft Skills 63
Appendix: Mozilla Universal Badges **64**
Appendix: Survey **66**
Appendix: Resources **69**
   Planning Stage 69
   Building Stage 70
   Presenting Stage 70
   Validation Stage 71

INTRODUCTION

A skill is an attribute required to complete a particular task. Some skills are transferable across subjects and disciplines. Traditional transferable skills are ones that are already commonly used in the workplace, such as professional writing or research and analysis. Emerging transferable skills are ones that will be in high demand in the near future, such as computational thinking, new media literacy, and transdisciplinarity.[1] Some technical skills are unique to a particular discipline. Often these technical skills can be further categorized by sub-skills that represent specific languages or technologies. For example, website design is a technical skill, and sub-skills for website design represent the different languages a professional might employ, such as HTML, CSS, and ASP.NET. Another distinction with skills includes those that relate to emotional value (personality traits, social graces, communication, etc.) – *soft skills* – and those that relate to rational value (quantifiable capabilities) – *hard skills*.[2] All *soft skills* are also transferable, *hard skills* can be technical or transferable. The importance in developing soft skills is often overlooked by aspiring professionals, however, are critical to becoming successful in most professions; soft skills often have more of an influence on success than hard skills. According to *Emotional Intelligence 2.0*, EQ (a measure of emotional intelligence) accounts for "fifty-eight percent of performance in all type of jobs."[3]

Skill sets are a combination of technical and transferable skills. Skill sets are utilized in professional-oriented web services; LinkedIn and MonsterJobs have made them a focal point of their profiles and built sophisticated searches based on them. A personal website should support the presentation and validation of skill sets. Using these web services, your skill set is accessible to a target audience (other professionals who benefit from knowing your functional capabilities). You want a potential employer, client, or partner to review your skill set. There are different ways to present your skill set, but in general, you create a list of skills from a standardized catalog and provide an assessment of your level of expertise with each skill. Providing a personal reference or endorsement validates your experience in applying the skill.

There are many benefits of publishing a skill set on professional and networking services. First and foremost, skill sets are effective criteria for external searches. A recruiter can search a skill set from a pool of thousands of potential candidates and retrieve a LinkedIn profile, a MonsterJobs résumé, or a professional-oriented website. Second, it is a standardized way to make comparisons between different candidates; educational institutions, companies, and professionals universally agree on the definitions of skills. The structure and format of a résumé is standardized, but the content is not standardized. Third, skills can be tagged to content in a similar way that keywords are tagged to blog content. This makes internal searches effective; someone can search on a skill and retrieve all the content related to the skill from the platform he or she is utilizing. Fourth, it is possible to plan the development and validation of a skill set; this is much more precise than planning degrees and actual careers. For example, imagine you plan to develop the skill of web design and later earn a certification in PHP (a web design language). You take an online course for two months and prepare for and take a certification test; it costs you a couple hundred dollars and takes a few months. This is far more efficient and practical than planning to earn a degree in computer science, which might take a few years and tens of thousands of dollars. Finally, in theory, a skill set is portable across web services and platforms. A professional keeps the same skill set in his or her LinkedIn profile, MonsterJobs profile/résumé, and personal website. (Though the infrastructure to publish a single skill set for multiple platforms has not been developed yet).

The traditional way of sending a résumé to a corporate website or through an online job board has become inefficient. For many job opportunities, there is a significant increase in the number of applicants submitting résumés, in part because it is easy to submit a résumé—both CareerBuilder and MonsterJobs have one-click submission buttons. Some companies have built résumé scanners that provide an initial screening from a large pool of résumés, but this has proven to be ineffective. It does not make sense to rule out potential candidates based on the frequency and occurrence of particular buzzwords. Furthermore, after they get past the first screening, they still have to comb through a collection of résumés.

A skill set makes the process a bit easier. It is possible to make an initial screening based on a skill set: a list of skills and a related level of expertise needed to perform a given task. With a search mechanism in place, a recruiter can make adjustments as he or she searches on a desired skill set to match the opportunity. After the initial screening, the recruiter can further narrow down the candidates by following up with the candidates' validation of their skills: checking references, viewing certifications, and reviewing samples of work. Once they have narrowed the pool of candidates to something manageable, the recruiters can review the content of a résumé or personal website.

In the future, corporations and recruiters will find most of their talent by actively searching their skill set—which is far more efficient and effective. This is a growing trend. One of LinkedIn's biggest revenue generators comes from its flagship product, Recruiter—which is a search engine to search on skill sets and other semantics to retrieve profiles.[4] Likewise, Monster built its own search engine called Power Resume, where recruiters can search on a skill set and retrieve a résumé. According to their 2011 annual report, bookings for this service increased roughly 30 percent over the previous year.[5] Skill sets are the backbone of recruiter searches.

Basing your career planning and development on a skill set is compelling for a few reasons. First, requirements for some careers are changing at breakneck speeds because of advancements in technology, so it makes sense to manage these requirements with specific skills rather than the nebulous degree. Second, it is important to have skills transferable across disciplines and subjects, where future demand is predictable. Third, professionals experience many career changes—on average seven in a lifetime[6]—so a skill set gives the opportunity to evaluate their options and plan their next move efficiently. Finally, professionals should strive to become experts, so they must learn and build an expertise with their skill set and then validate whenever possible. Taking the time to validate a skill set will strengthen a résumé. It is a worthwhile time investment because it takes much less time to merely validate a skill than it does to build it. One of the biggest features that LinkedIn added to their website is the concept of skills and a sophisticated endorsement interface to validate them.

A skills-based approach is the development of a skill set in four stages: planning, building, presenting, and validating. These stages are sequential for each skill, though the path can be reevaluated and modified at any time. The beauty of a skills-based approach is its simplicity and flexibility. It effectively handles the complex factors in career planning and development, such as changing career demands due to technology and demographics, rising education costs, and increasingly competitive employment market.

This book guides you through planning a skill set to achieve career aspirations, learning and building skill expertise, responding to setbacks and opportunities, presenting skills on various platforms, and validating skills to establish credibility with your intended audience. The objective of this book is to provide a framework that can be used throughout your career to increase your chances of success. Career planning is the key to finding happiness. A survey was conducted to establish whether this proposed methodology is practical and effective, and the results are presented in the book.

SKILLS-BASED APPROACH

Establishing a skill set over time should be a primary goal of every professional. The definition of a skill set is the combination of skills you have acquired throughout your employment, education, and other experiences. A skill is an attribute required to complete a particular task. Some skills include business analysis, professional writing, project management, graphic design, website design, and application development. Developing your skill set occurs in four progressive stages: planning, building, presenting, and validating.

The first stage of a skills-based approach is the planning stage. There are two objectives during this stage. First, you identify what skills to include in a desired skill set. This list includes skills that not only demonstrate competency but also help you achieve a desired career path. Second, once you have a skill set, you plan actions to learn and build an expertise with the skills. If you are a college student, this might include taking a course, applying for an internship, or joining an extracurricular activity. If you are an early career professional, this might include taking on a particular project at work or joining an organization; you might join Toastmasters to develop the skill of public speaking, for example. The result of the planning stage is an effective short-term guide and a long-term proposal. Planning is an ongoing process, so you will frequently reevaluate and change the plan based on your experiences.

The second stage of a skills-based approach is the building stage. During this stage, you assess your aptitude to learn skills, optimize your learning experience, and decide on the next course of action. As you learn skills, it is necessary to evaluate your capabilities each step of the way. Learning a skill can be time-consuming, unpleasant, and costly, so it is not worth expending all these resources when you may not have a favorable outcome. The three ways to create an ideal learning environment are to *set the stage* with your supervisor or professor, find a mentor, and learn methodologies (practiced ways to apply a skill). Once you complete an action, decide on your next course of action: find other ways to learn a skill, discover ways to advance your expertise, or drop the skill from your skill set. This will continually build expertise with a skill set throughout your career.

Once you have established a footprint with your desired skill set, you start the third stage of a skills-based approach: the presenting stage. The objective of this stage is to publish your skill set to a target audience: associates, clients, recruiters, and/or partners. You want to have your skill set (a representation of your functional capabilities) accessible to everyone in your target audience. Theoretically, there are five ways you can present a skill: **tagging, listing, explaining, demonstrating, and summarizing.** The functionality of the platform you are publishing to will determine which way you present your skill set.

The final stage of a skills-based approach is the validation stage. Recently, the concept of validating a skill was reserved for highly specialized professionals. Since it is easy to do and accessible to your counterparts, however, it is now a requirement for all professionals. The easiest way to validate skills is by having a reference or endorsement on your behalf; LinkedIn has made the process of getting your skills endorsed automatic. LinkedIn claims to have one billion endorsements on their network.[7] According to a recent survey, providing a sample of work is the most effective way to validate your skills.[8] It allows for you to demonstrate your expertise and for someone to make his or her own assessment of your credibility. Lastly most professions have ways to earn certifications, awards, or licenses that validate skills related to them.

The development of your skill set should be a lifelong commitment. It challenges you to continually improve while reevaluating who you are and what exactly you want to achieve with your career. It is a fluid process in which you can change course at any time, and, rather than getting caught up with the difficulties and expense of acquiring new degrees, you can pinpoint precisely what skills you need to best move forward.

Planning Stage

One of the most important advantages in adopting the skills-based approach is planning what you want to achieve with your career. Unfortunately, most young professionals do not set aside time to consider their career aspirations; this might be part of the reason professionals change careers so often. Your career is not only about making money but is a source of happiness and an opportunity to make art.[9] A *Harvard Business Review* article defines *thriving* as the key to career happiness. There are two components of thriving: vitality, the "sense of being alive, passionate, and excited" and learning, "the growth that comes from gaining new knowledge and skills."[10] Because career planning is so important, a large part of this chapter is dedicated to career-planning approaches—where you take an introspective look at inner motivations, passions, and strengths, and then translate the results into a skill set. The chapter concludes with a short discussion on different actions you might choose in order to learn and build a skill.

During the planning stage, you derive a list of skills you will need to pursue your career aspirations. This is no different than any other type of career planning, although once you decide what you want to do, you translate what you have into skills. The following discussion is centered on four ways to plan your career: craftsman mind-set, passion theory, product to market, and self-awareness. The idea is not to choose one way over another, but rather to consider using advantages from each of them as you plan your career.

Planning Your Career

Craftsman Mindset[1]
Focus on what value you are producing in your job, and build your career around it

Product to Market
Consider yourself as a product, and potential employers as consumers.

There is no magic formula, where you weigh each factor and come up with an exact, set-in-stone career plan. Combine the benefits of each as you plan your career.

Passion Theory
First figure out what you're passionate about, and then find a job that matches this passion.

Self Awareness
Take a personality and/or strengths test, then plan your career based on the results.

1) Cal Newport, *So Good They Can't Ignore You* (New York: Hachett, 2012).

Craftsman's Mindset

In the book *So Good They Can't Ignore You: Why Skills Trump Passion in the Quest for Work You Love*, Cal Newport defines and argues his perspective on planning your career: the *craftsman's mindset*.[11] With the craftsman's mindset, you identify your core competencies—skills that differentiate you from others and that you have an innate understanding of and commitment to develop. Moreover, you focus on what value you produce in your job, and become "so good they can't ignore you." As you develop these skills, you invest in your own "career capital"—something you can draw on for the rest of your life.

In most situations, a craftsman's mindset is more beneficial than basing your plan on passion because you increase your chances of success considerably when your talents are a deciding factor in your career plans. There is clarity in planning how you build an expertise with your skill set; you build your "career capital." To the contrary, there are no guarantees of success when you take on the passion approach. That can set you up for failure and disillusionment, and very few of us have a lifelong passion that guides us through difficult career decisions for the rest of our lives. To build his argument, Cal Newport identifies three traits that define great work:

- o Creativity: demonstrating the ability to formulate new ideas.
- o Impact: reaching out to your audience and making a difference.
- o Control: understanding what needs to be done, and having the power to do it.

None of these traits are rooted in passion, but rather in career capital—the results of practicing and nurturing your skill set over many years. You must develop a mastery of your skill set before really experiencing these traits. Furthermore, you feel self-efficacy in creating something of value; you are not necessarily driven by financial gain or prestige.[12]

In the book *Drive*, Larry Bird discusses how he used "deliberate practice" to take his basketball skills to another level.[13] He started playing basketball because of his passion for the game, but early on understood that he had exceptional skill in shooting the basketball, so he invested in his "career capital." He practiced shooting a basketball at every possible opportunity, whether it was before and after team practices or at his home. Larry was exceptional in all facets of the game of basketball, but he will be remembered particularly for his amazing free-throw and three-point shooting accuracy. (His lifetime free-throw average in the NBA was 88.6 percent, and he led the league four times according to his Wikipedia page.) He incessantly practiced shooting a basketball his entire life. Larry Bird says, "A winner is someone who recognizes his God-given talents, works his tail off to develop them into skills, and uses these skills to accomplish his goals."

A problem with the craftsman's mindset is that most people do not have core competencies that can propel them through a career. Cal Newport discusses situations of professionals who went to an Ivy League school or have an amazing talent. Many of us are average, however, and do not have the advantage of landing a position that fits in nicely with advancing our skills. Perhaps the only option is to find employment that satisfies our immediate lifestyle needs. If you do not have any core competencies, you must plan your skill set on another theory (passion theory, product to market, or self-awareness).

Passion Theory

Popular career advice given by career counselors is to follow your dreams or to follow something you are passionate about—to self-reflect and identify subject matter that drives you. The passion theory suggests planning your career around a passion, an inner motivation, or a desire to do something. The assumption is that your pent-up passion will drive you to succeed. However, there are three problems with betting your future on this approach. First, no matter how passionate you are about a subject or discipline, there are no guarantees you will succeed. Becoming an astronaut is one of the most popular *dream professions*, however, it also one of the most selective professions; since 1959, only 330 candidates have been selected for Astronaut Candidate training program.[14] No matter how passionate you are about becoming an astronaut, the odds of becoming one are stacked against you. Second, many of us never find a passionate career pursuit. You have to be exposed to something and show self-efficacy before any passion takes root. Third, it is easy to spend a lot of time thinking about a dream job because you are passionate but then not effectively plan the necessary steps to make it happen. In *Top Dog*, a book about competition, Po Branson discusses the results of a study by Gabriele Oettingen: "When job seekers spend time visualizing their dream job, two years later they are less likely to have found employment in any job. (If they someday do find a job, it will be for lower pay and lower recognition than the jobs held by those who had spent less time daydreaming about their career.)"[15]

Self-exploring subjects and disciplines that you might be passionate about is a worthwhile endeavor, and understanding the underlying themes that make you happy makes you wiser. But if you do decide to follow a passion in choosing a career, you should consider the following points before making any commitments.

Do you have the necessary skill set? It is crucial to make an initial assessment whether you have the capability to learn the skills necessary to follow your passion because if you do not, you should not make learning them a career pursuit. Many professionals have the passion to be a leader, but most do not have the necessary skills to become one, and not everyone can be a leader.

Reassess yourself each step of the way. If you cannot differentiate yourself from others in the same field or are not effectively learning the skills, you must focus your efforts on something else. It might be difficult to drop a passion after you have already invested time into learning it, so you may want to channel your passion in ways other than a career pursuit. College freshman flock to computer-programming degrees because they are enticed by technology and the abundance of opportunities when they graduate. The first few classes you take in a computer science degree are difficult math courses and theoretical programming courses, and by design they weed out students who will probably not get the coveted computer science degree. Learning skills is a significant investment, so you should cut your losses as soon as possible if you are assured of not succeeding.

Do not internalize failure. One reason why Cal Newport (in *So Good They Can't Ignore You*) advises against pursuing a career based on passion is because if you do not succeed, you are left with discontent and disillusionment. You will ask yourself, Why did I not succeed? What should I do now? Becoming a doctor is a popular career pursuit, but getting into medical school is astonishingly difficult—fewer than 9 percent of medical school applications were accepted in 2011.[16] For the thousands of pre-med graduates who were not accepted to medical school, it is self-defeating to think of their undergraduate degree as a total waste. To overcome this rejection, they should find ways to leverage their current skill set to find other opportunities; consider other medical related occupations that do not require a medical degree, such as selling pharmaceutical equipment. This is an advantage of a skills-based approach: when you think of your professional background as a skill set, you can absorb setbacks by taking your current skills and constructing a plan to move forward.

The passion is not all about you. You want to find a career that adds value to those around you, so you make a positive contribution. It is not all about making you happy. For example, say you have a passion for teaching high school math; you have a strong aptitude for math, however, you cannot engage a classroom of students – they do not understand your examples and find you boring. Instead of forcing your passion on others where it impedes their growth (in this case, learning math properly), you should find another career where you can best use your skills.

Do not sacrifice a stable lifestyle. If you have a stable lifestyle with your current career, you should not drop what you are doing unless you can be assured you can harbor a failure in the pursuit of your passion. You do not want to jeopardize your well-being because of a career passion. Possible barriers in following a passion might be the financial cost of taking courses or simply the loss of income from not continuing your current job. When you provide for a family, it is difficult to decide to go back to college for a degree.

Sometimes the Passion Theory Works

There are times when the passion theory works. Sometimes you identify a talent you are passionate about at an early age and then spend the rest of your life mastering it; many famous musicians spend their entire life developing their skill of composing. Sometimes you identify a passion later in your career then figure out ways to pursue it. Being passionate about your career can bring lasting happiness, so you might want to pursue a career based on passion.

Sometimes your passion may be drawn from your strongest talents. Joan recognized her skill of drawing while she was a young girl in her art classes, and being an artist became her lifelong passion. She went to college for art studio, and then joined organizations to develop her amazing talent. During her career, she started to travel the world, and it became another passion of hers. Although it did not replace her passion as an artist, but rather transformed it, she now had new, unexplored subject matter: landscapes of her world travels. You can identify your passion at an early age, and develop the necessary skills, and sometimes you might add dimensions to your skills by incorporating experiences from other areas of your life. Becoming a master of your skill can be a lifelong endeavor.

Jeff majored in business and excelled in it. He made Dean's List every semester in his academic career. After graduation, he landed a high-paying job for one of the top management-consulting firms in the DC area. Following his wife's tracks, he moved back to his hometown and got a job with a reputable bank. After a couple of years, he decided his passion was teaching physical education—probably spurred from his wife being a teacher, as well as his love of sports—so he quit his job and enrolled at a local college to get his teaching certification. He happily has been teaching physical education for more than a decade. Keep an open mind, and self-reflect as you navigate through your career because you might have the opportunity to follow a passion that had not presented itself earlier.

Jeff's experience satisfied the five requirements for taking on a career passion. First, he had the capacity to learn the necessary skills to become certified in education. Second, while taking classes, he performed well by getting good grades, and, more importantly, became creative and thought about what he was learning outside of the classroom. Third, he never experienced failure—though he was tested when he faced a highly competitive job market for teachers after he graduated. Fourth, he made strong connections with the kids he taught during his initial placements. Finally, he never sacrificed losing his stable lifestyle. When he quit his job and enrolled to become a teacher, his wife was gainfully employed, and he had put away extra money to help pay for his education.

Product to Market

With the product-to-market approach, you think of yourself as a product and potential employers as consumers. You market your personal brand in the same way that companies promote their brand: create brand awareness, find product differentiation, use all types of media, develop a marketing pitch, and understand your target market. This career-planning approach has a major external factor: the target market. Consider the following elements as you develop your personal brand for your target market.

Understand who you are and who you want to be. Use self-evaluation to identify who you are: your strengths, personality traits, inner motivations, and passions. Use the test results discussed below in the self-awareness section. Before you conceptualize how to deliver your services to a target market, you must understand what services you are selling.

Understand your target market. Do a quick supply-and-demand analysis for careers in the area you want to work, and consider in which careers you have the best opportunity to succeed. Have a deep understanding of the influencers in the region you are targeting. For example, identify companies that are established or up-and-coming and how they might move your career forward. Tailor your personal brand to reach a target market in order to maximize your chances of success.

Create brand awareness. With social media and networks on the Internet, there are many ways to reach out to your target market: advertise your brand in social media, publish your résumé on job boards, and index a personal website in search engines. You can also create a blog and participate in blogs related to your targeted professions. Most professions have an umbrella organization that represents their interests and provides opportunities to network. Creating brand awareness influences how you plan to learn skills. For example, creating brand awareness might influence whether you take a course or internship and with what institutions you plan to create affiliations; a local university might have more clout than an equally ranked university farther away. One goal of taking on an internship is the prospect of the company offering you a position after you complete the internship. You sow the seeds of a relationship while you learn skills.

Find product differentiation, ways you separate your skill set from others. As you develop your personal brand, find ways to differentiate *you* from the *crowd*. Define skills you have experience in and that are short in supply in disciplines you are targeting, so you make your skills a precious commodity.[17] You want to be *the social media marketer* or *the inspiring presenter* or *the professional writer* or *the front-end web developer*. The idea is to carve out a niche within an ecosystem that has clearly defined boundaries: where you live, what college you earned a degree from, and whom you know (and there may be other ones). So for career planning, you want to identify how you can make a unique contribution to a predefined ecosystem.

Develop a marketing pitch. Imagine a problem and explain how you solve the problem and include a value proposition.[18] Create a marketing message that conveys your unique strengths. The marketing message is essentially a forecast of where you want to be at some point in the future, and having this vision will help you plan and develop the necessary skill set.

With the product-to-market approach, you create a marketing plan to reach your career objectives. You consider the appropriate target market and develop a personal brand to give you the best opportunity of success. Career planning involves identifying what skills differentiate you from your competitors, so it does not necessarily mean developing skills related to core competencies or passions. The product-to-market approach is a practical way to plan a career, especially if you need to find employment and cannot afford to be particular.

In *Me 2.0*, Dan Schwabel, a preeminent writer on the subject of personal branding, discusses how to create a marketing strategy as you plan your career. He dedicates a few chapters discussing how to develop a marketing plan and identify your short- and long-term goals.[19] Although, for the purposes of career planning with a skills-based approach, the idea is to take the results of the marketing plan and translate them into the skills you will need to reach these short- and long-term goals. This marketing plan will also influence your action plan for developing skills because the actions you employ affects the connections, relationships, and credibility you need to reach career aspirations.

Self-Awareness

The premise of the self-awareness approach in career planning is to understand your personality traits, strengths, values, and interests through testing, and then use the results to plan your career. It makes sense to be self-aware while making career-planning decisions. In fact, elements of the self-awareness approach are in each of the other approaches: leveraging core competencies—your top few strengths—is suggested in the craftsman mindset; differentiating strengths and personality traits is suggested in the product-to-market approach; and following your values and interests is suggested in the passion approach.

Taking these self-awareness tests is becoming more popular because they are easily accessible on the Internet and are relatively cheap. Considering how important career planning should be, there are no good reasons why you should not take them. There are many different types of tests and assessments offered with various services. Three of these tests are discussed below: a Gallup strengths test, a MyPlan personality test, and a MyPlan interests test.

Gallup offers a well-conceived service based on an online strengths test; it is stimulating to affirm your dominant strengths, learn about your hidden strengths, and find your weaknesses. A couple things make the results of this test very powerful. The report clarifies precisely what you should be doing; it is something you can share with supervisors, teammates, and colleagues so they know how you can make the biggest impact. You can use the results to plan how you want to develop the related skills in your skill set. Using the results correlates with the craftsman's approach in career planning; the highest-ranked strengths are your "career capital"—something you should commit to developing for the rest of your life.

MyPlan.com offers a personality test based on Carl Jung's publication *Psychological Types*. The test results include four of your personality preferences (with a four-letter acronym) and, more importantly, to what degree you favor one trait over its complement. For example, if you slightly favor being an introvert versus and extrovert, then public speaking might be something you can overcome without too much effort; otherwise it might be very difficult. Taking this type of personality test is useful in determining a broad scope of skills to consider while developing your career pursuit. It is also more traditional, so it does not necessarily favor higher-skilled professions.

MyPlan.com also offers a test they call an interests inventory. The test results identify primary and secondary interest areas (based on Dr. Holland's theory): realistic, investigative, artistic, social, enterprising, and conventional. These primary and secondary interest areas provide a basic understanding of what careers might interest you.

It is advantageous to understand who you are and who you want to be as you plan your career. Why tread against your internal self? You should avoid presentational speaking if you are a strong introvert. If your strengths are learning and ideation, you should plan a career where you are constantly being stimulated with new ideas, otherwise you will probably not find career happiness.

Career-Planning Takeaways

Planning out your career is a difficult undertaking because there are many factors to consider. Nevertheless, it is something you should do because it can help bring you happiness, security, motivation, direction, and success. During the planning, focus on the development of a skill set that will enable you to reach your career goals. Career planning is meant to be fluid, so you can reassess and change your plan as you encounter obstacles or opportunities.

In developing your skill set, you should consider the takeaways from each career-planning approach as you develop your career plan. When there is conflict, weigh your opportunity to succeed as the primary concern. Taken together, the results paint a holistic view of you and possible opportunities: realistic short-term prospects, potential long-term pursuits, and fallback options.

Translating Planning Results to Skills

As you work through the different career-planning approaches, the next step is to translate the results of your career planning into a desired skill set. Depending on the career-planning approaches you utilize, there are a variety of factors to work with, including personality traits, strengths, core competencies, careers, and inner motivations. Translating these factors to skills should be straightforward, though at times it might seem like you are going back-and-forth between defining careers and the skills related to them. Below is a table that depicts how this translation works.

Career Approach	Career-Planning Takeaway	Translating to Skills	Example
Self-Awareness	Personality Traits	Personality traits are broad in nature, so many skills can be identified for each trait, and how well you perform each skill is more uncertain.	***Judger (Carl Jung personality preference)*** Business Management, Project Management, Virtual Collaboration, Design Mindset
Self-Awareness, Craftsman Mindset, Product to Market	Strengths, Core Competencies (top-ranked strengths)	Sometimes strengths will be defined in the same level of detail as a skill; otherwise, identify skills that correlate with the strength.	***Learner (a strength from Gallup)*** Research and Analysis, Sense-Making, Computational Thinking
Self-Awareness, Passion Theory, Product to Market	Careers	Research what skills are needed for the career. Check job descriptions of the career in job boards. Check websites of organizations that represent the profession. Get advice from a career counselor or someone who has the career.	***Free-Lance Web Developer*** Web Development, Database Design, Graphic Design, Programming
Self-Awareness, Passion Theory	Inner Motivations	Identify the skills needed to succeed with an inner-motivation or passion.	***"Motivated to get funding for non-profits"*** Grant Writing, Accounting, Research and Analysis

There are advantages in working with skill sets as you plan your career. First, there is a need to be fluent with your career planning because of the rapid changes in technology and demographics. Developing a skill set with transferable skills—skills that can be applied across disciplines and subject matter —prepares you for changes in careers you are targeting. Second, you can plan more accurately the learning and building of an expertise of a skill (as opposed to a career). Then you can develop your skill set in a logical progression throughout your career: planning, building, presenting, and validating (according to the skills-based approach).

Career-Planning Considerations

Planning your career is challenging because there are so many factors—some of them are professional and others are personal. In fact, some counselors downplay the whole idea of career planning for this reason. While you are career planning, you should consider three issues: ever-changing career responsibilities due to rapid changes in technology and demographics, the need to have a holistic plan that addresses your personal life, and the hidden value in being spontaneous. Planning the development of a skill set mitigates the effect of some of these issues.

Some counselors argue it is too difficult to predict the demand for careers and their responsibilities too far in the future. Part of this is because of how quickly technologies are being adopted. For example, by 2016, almost 92 percent of mid-sized companies plan to invest in cloud computing[20]—a technology that was first introduced only a couple of years ago. Any careers related to hosting websites on servers will experience a very different landscape in providing their service, and professionals will have to train to use the new technology. Part of the difficulty is planning for changes in demographics; our population is getting older, people are moving to cities, and areas are becoming hubs for particular services or industries. The younger generation will have to support the older generation, and the older generation will have an increasingly later retirement age. Where you want to live and work will play a role in your career plans; perhaps you want to live where you grew up or went to college. And for many careers, location is key, such as application development in Silicon Valley or financial analysis in New York. In a *Harvard Business Review* article, "Career Plans Are Dangerous,"[21] a team of writers summarizes why career planning can seem imprecise:

> "If you don't know what the world is going to look like five years from now, there is not a lot of sense trying to predict potential external factors planning your career based on that dubious prediction."

As you learn transferable skills, you invest in a basic foundation that you can build on as you respond to changes in career requirements; you are equipped to learn the intricacies of a new technology.

Career planning discussed up to this point does not take into account the importance of being happy outside of work, having strong family and community ties. In his article, "How Will You Measure Your Life,"[22] Clayton M. Christensen talks about the importance of three themes in your career: having fulfilling work, maintaining a strong family, and keeping your integrity. The latter two themes have not been discussed in the career-planning approaches, but should be taken into account. You should consider how your career affects your family. If you are raising children, then you probably should not consider being an entry–level investment banker (analysts can routinely expect to work ninety to one hundred hours per week or more[23]). For Christensen, much of his integrity is rooted in his strong religious faith, and he argues that you should not be forced to do something against your beliefs. (He uses not playing in a championship basketball game on Sunday as an example.) Your principles should not be compromised in any way as you plan your career. Christensen says about principles, "It's easier to hold to your principles 100 percent of the time than it is to hold on to them 98 percent of the time."

When you make a career transition, you should consider how it would affect all aspects of your life. A skills-based approach is based on your skill set—not actual occupations or careers—so you have flexibility. As you narrow down opportunities, you should "set the stage" with a potential employer by telling them your expectations and asking them about your commitment. Let them know if you cannot stay after 5:00 p.m. because you need to be with your family. Learn about their corporate culture, and make sure it is in sync with your principles.

Being spontaneous can make your career an adventure and lead to success. The best example of acting on spontaneity is an e-entrepreneur, which is simply an entrepreneur that offers Internet-related services. To be successful, an e-entrepreneur has to accurately assess an opportunity and pounce on it; there is no time to mull over an opportunity with the fast pace of the Internet. There can be some planning, but much of the initial momentum will be based on instinct. Most people do not plan to be e-entrepreneurs because you must have an innovative idea to become one.

A skills-based approach suggests developing a skill set over time, so as you build your skill set, you can always reassess and change your plan mid-flight. It is meant to be flexible in order to respond to external factors. Perhaps you come up with an innovative idea and want to move on it; you can rely on the skills you have been building for the past ten years as you change your career path to launch this idea. In this way, basing your career plan on the development of a skill set still leaves you the opportunity to be spontaneous.

Developing an Action Plan

Once you derive a list of skills that comprise your skill set, you create an action plan to learn and develop an expertise with each skill. The biggest factor in mapping out an action plan is what stage you are in your career. If you are or will be a student, the actions include taking courses, interning, and joining clubs or organizations. If you are a professional, the actions include taking on a project, training, doing an apprenticeship, reading a book, volunteering, and taking a course. To understand the best ways learn skills, seek guidance from a career counselor, mentor, or someone who has the career you are pursuing. They can steer you in the right direction. You can also find books, blogs, and organizations that provide information about disciplines and subjects you are interested in.

In a survey about a skills-based approach (referred to earlier), a question was posed regarding the effectiveness of learning a skill with the various actions mentioned above. Taking on a project at work is by far the best way to build a skill according to the survey. In fact, only one respondent reported it ineffective, and eighty-seven percent reported it as a "very effective" way to build a skill. This has a few implications. If you are a student, find an internship to practice the skills you are learning in your courses. If you are currently looking for employment, search for a job or an apprenticeship that builds your desired skill set. Perhaps your only objective is to learn skills so the job/apprenticeship is a stepping-stone to something more long term in the future. If you are employed, be assertive and take on a project that builds your skill set; for example, tell your supervisors why you want to make a presentation or be the lead developer on a project.

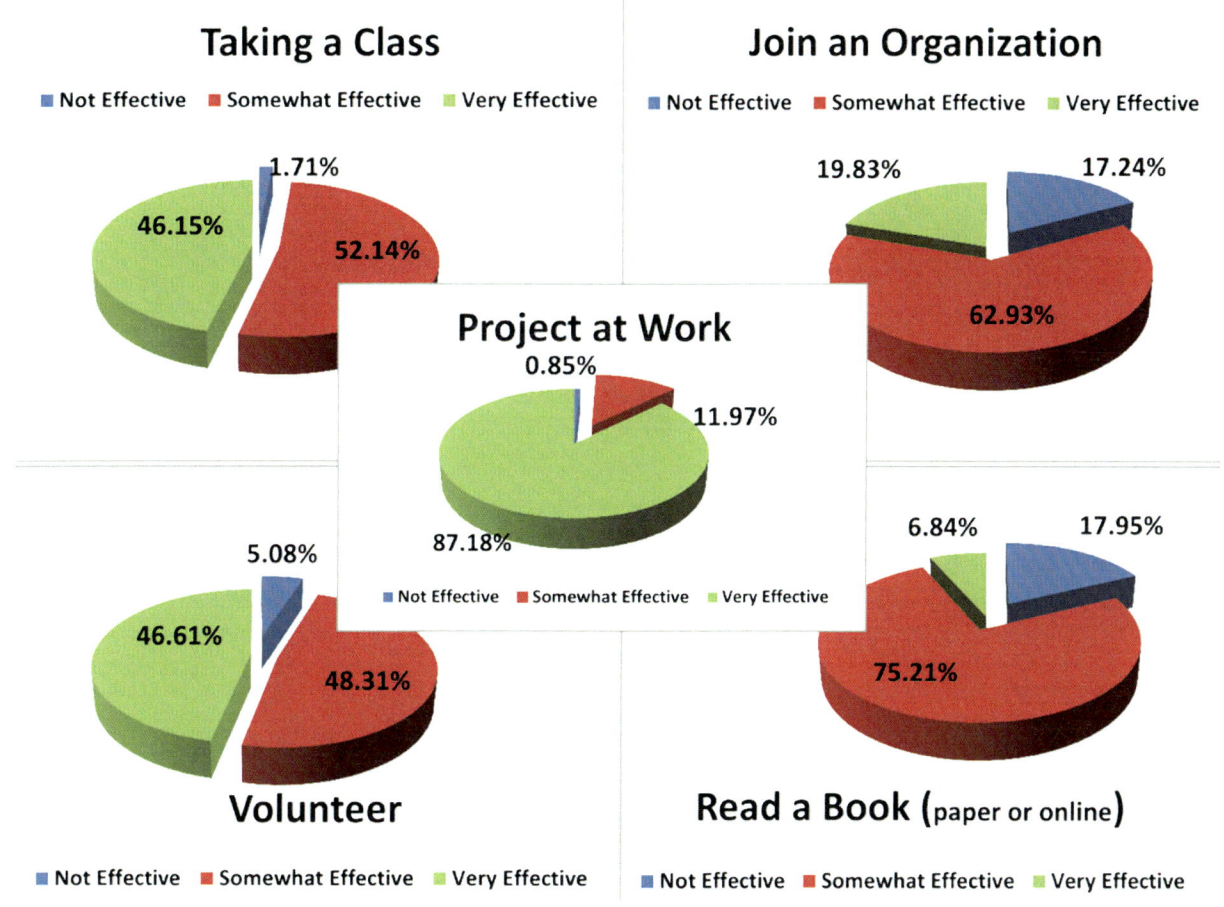

The effectiveness of taking a class and volunteering also elicited a strong favorable response; only a few respondents thought taking a class or volunteering were ineffective (two percent and five percent, respectively). An advantage with these methods is that they often can be addressed with few prerequisites; you do not have to get hired for a job or be accepted to take on a project. The disadvantage of both, however, is that they require a commitment of time outside of your paying job, and you usually have to pay for classes.

Most of the respondents thought that joining an organization or reading a book are "somewhat effective." Books are sometimes the easiest, cheapest way to learn a new skill—especially learning a new programming language or technology.

Building Stage

Equipped with a plan (from the planning stage), you enter into the building stage of the skills-based approach – this is where you learn and build an expertise with each skill in your skill set. You might be a student or an entry-level or mid-career professional, so you could be taking different actions to learn skills. During the building stage, you assess how well you are learning skills, communicate with your supervisors regarding what you want to accomplish, find a mentor to help you move forward, discover methodologies or practiced ways to apply a skill, and make decisions on a next step for developing skills.

Skills-Based Approach

Use Assessments
Self-assessment, peer review, course grade, employment evaluation, online badge.

Communicate With Supervisor
"Set the Stage," discuss career goals and expectations.

Seek out a Mentor
A fast track to learn skills, get direct feedback, find your best advocate.

Learn Methodologies
Learn ways to apply a skill from experts who practice them.

Use a Diary
Something you can refer to when you present your skill set.

Decide on Next Step
Figure ways to advance your expertise or other ways to learn it.

Building Stage

This is where you learn and build an expertise with a skill set.

As you build an expertise with skills, it is crucial to understand how well you are learning them through assessments. There are a few types of assessments: a self-assessment, a formal or informal employment evaluation, a grade for a project or course, a team evaluation, or the results from a certification or test. The assessment you use depends on how you are learning a skill.

Whether you are taking a class or doing a project at work, you should communicate to your professor or supervisor, and let them know what you are trying to accomplish with your skill set. This is especially important when you are starting new employment; it sets the stage for growth with a new employer. The reason for reaching out to the actual people you will be working with is two-fold. First, you want to optimize your work environment to learn and build an expertise with skills. They can assign projects to you, set you up with a mentor, and provide you with feedback. Second, you sow the seeds of a relationship. There is a strong possibility that these same people you are working with now will later become a reference who will be asked to testify on your behalf.

It is important to seek out a mentor who can guide you through learning skills and give immediate, candid feedback each step of the way. If you find a mentor, the contribution to your career development is immeasurable; learning from a master might be the fastest way to develop your skill set.

There are usually many ways to apply a skill, so it is worth knowing different methodologies for a particular skill. Some methodologies are obvious because you are required to use them. You might have to prepare a report, name files, or program a certain way. Some methodologies are subtle, like a thought process to solve a problem; you have to be observant and inquisitive to learn these types of methodologies properly. As you become an expert with your skill set, you will have a collection of methodologies—some your own and some borrowed.

You should keep a weekly diary as you build your skill set. In the diary, keep track of your progress with learning the skills (if you have reached measurable goals), provide context on how you are applying the skills, and highlight any milestones, all of which you can refer to later when you present your skill set with a personal website. It is also important to record all of your skill-set assessments.

Assessments

One of the most important aspects of the building stage in a skills-based approach is to assess how well you are learning or building an expertise with your skill set. As you execute the actions from your skill set plan, you assess your capabilities of learning the skills and make decisions based on your assessments. Depending on the type of action you are using to learn a skill, making an assessment can be easy. For example, if you are taking a course, your assessment is simply the grade you got on a paper or the course itself. In other circumstances, such as learning web development from a book, you may have to self-reflect and make your own assessment. In a *Harvard Business Review* article, Amy Gallo says, "To move from experimentation to mastery, you need to reflect on what you are learning."[24]

Self-assessments are difficult because they require evaluating yourself objectively. There are two different types of self-assessments, a reflective assessment and a forecast assessment. When you reflect on past experiences, you make an assessment regarding how well you applied particular skills. It is easy to be too critical or to embellish how well you performed a given task. This is why you should have measurable goals to anchor the assessment. Forecasting how you will perform in applying skills is more difficult because you might have little experience to base your assessment on. Moreover, you might not have time to think and respond: a supervisor might ask you whether you can take on the role of a project manager, for example.

Formal employment evaluations are a common way employers gauge your performance while working for them; they can be conducted on a quarterly, bi-annual, or annual basis. You should have a meeting with your supervisors to discuss the results if it is not already part of the process, and make sure your discussion is centered on how well you are learning your skill set. If your employer does not have a formal employment evaluation, suggest having an **informal employment evaluation** where you meet with your immediate supervisor to get as much feedback as possible on your skill set.

A grade for a course or project can be used to evaluate how well you are learning skills if you are a student. A grade is an effective assessment because it is an objective measurement across a pool of students; professors are ethically required to assign grades that accurately reflect a student's work product. If you have any questions about a grade, you should meet with your professors to discuss what you do not understand. Ask for their suggestions regarding further development of your skills, so they can guide you to other resources. Professors are usually aware of the latest developments in skills and subjects related to their field, and would be happy to share that information. If you get a poor grade, you might want to ask your professor bluntly whether you have the aptitude to learn the subject matter; a reason for taking an assessment is to understand whether you have the capability to learn the skills in your planned skill set.

Take an online certification or assessment test. This is beneficial if you do not have another way to assess your learning of a skill. For example, if you read a book, there is no formal way to assess how well you process and practice the information you learned. The adoption of new technologies happens so quickly that often the only option is to read a book or take an online course. A certification or assessment test is an effective measure of your competency when you have to learn a skill quickly. And you might acquire an online badge to assess your level of expertise with a skill; this is especially useful when there are incremental levels such as novice, intermediate, and expert and there are no other ways to demonstrate competency.

A Peer Review is an assessment from another professional or student who is not necessarily more experienced than you. And in most cases, peer reviews are conducted by a group of like-minded professionals where you get feedback from more than one person. When you work in a team, peer reviews are the best assessment of your team-oriented skills. Peer reviews are commonly used in both educational and professional settings.

Setting the Stage

Setting the Stage with a New Employer

An Employer....

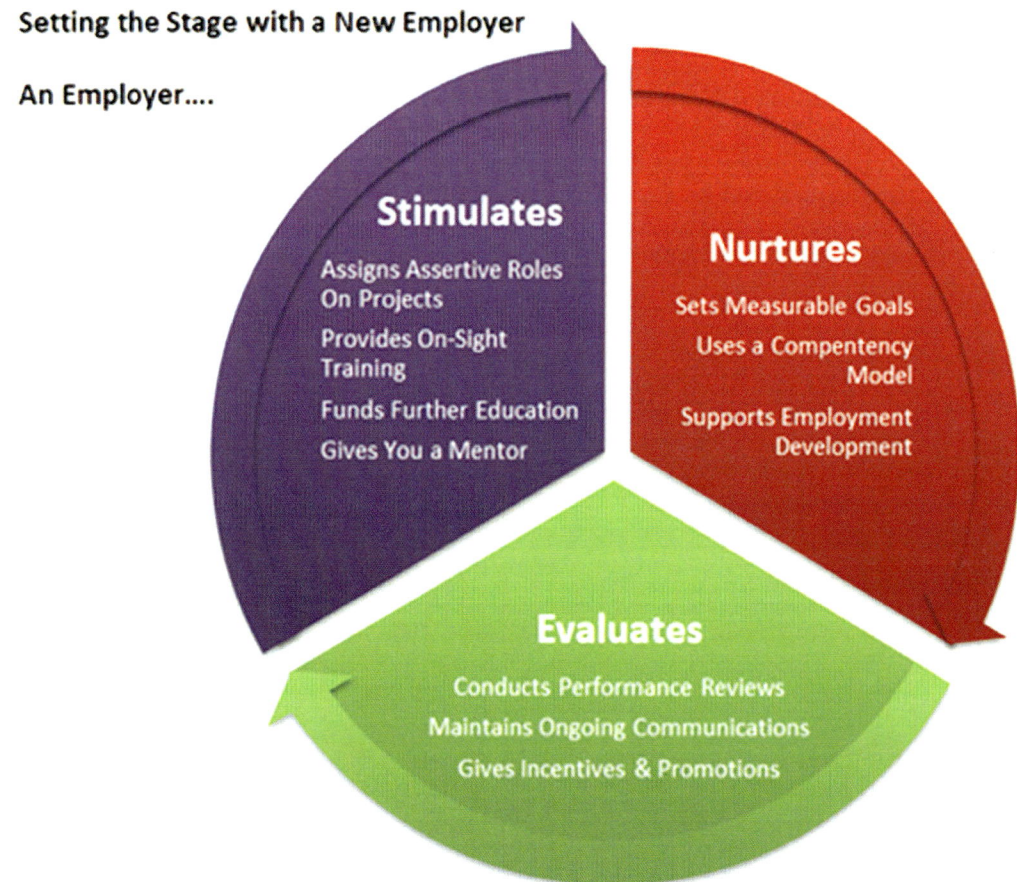

Whenever you begin a course, internship, or job, you should communicate exactly what you are trying to accomplish (in developing your skills), discover ways to build skills, learn about expectations and how they are measured, and start relationship building – this is "setting the stage". You optimize your chances of success by giving your employer the opportunity to guide you; there is a mutual understanding of expectations moving forward (which is far more effective than being retrospective).

Employers support the development of their employees' skills, especially if it increases productivity and quality of work. Some established employers understand the learning curve of their new hires, and therefore already provide the necessary training to help maximize their learning potential. This reinforces the idea of getting hired for your transferable and technical skills and then learning specific technologies or applications after you are employed. According to a 2012 study completed by Right Management, the demand for training workers with broad and specialized skills is "growing exponentially due to demand".[25] Startups most likely do not offer any training, so you may have to seek out off-site training such as a seminar, an online course, or a course at a local college. Again, most employers are willing to invest in their employees, so it is beneficial to ask if they will pay for training.

Making connections is becoming one of the biggest influencers of success. Social media makes it easy to establish connections and share these connections with the presentation of your profile. LinkedIn has transformed how we interact with connections and the process of being endorsed for skills by connections. All of your connections on LinkedIn have access to your list of skills and endorsements. Relationships are becoming increasingly important because spending so much time working with technology creates a hunger for personal human interaction. To complement their functional value, professionals need to shore up on their emotional value, which cannot be replicated by technology. There is a strong link between applying skills and the relationships you make through your experiences. Connections may endorse your level of expertise with skills, give you feedback on how well you are applying skills, participate with you in building skills, or teach you how to apply a skill. Whenever you start something new, you should start immediately building relationships.

It makes sense to be honest and direct regarding what you want to accomplish while working for an employer. There are clear benefits for an employer: by keeping you well incentivized, they can lessen the chance of your jumping at the next big opportunity. This is becoming more common; 84 percent of US employees planned to look for new jobs in 2011.[26]

When taking on a new opportunity, identify whether your employer has a goal-setting process, a competency model, performance reviews, and/or incentives or promotions for reaching their expectations.[27] Basically, you want to know if your employer provides their own type of assessment before you start working for them. As discussed earlier, you must use assessments to understand how well you are learning skills. The prospect of incentives such as increased pay might provide you with added motivation, and understanding what it takes to be promoted clarifies your employer's expectations for you take on a bigger role in their company. Getting a promotion might be a requirement to continue building an expertise with your skill set.

Finding a Mentor

Learning from a mentor is a powerful way to build an expertise with a skill for many reasons. First and foremost, you are a recipient of a wealth of knowledge from an interpersonal relationship; there is value in hearing candid responses and stories about a mentor's experiences—things not easily passed along in other ways. Second, they provide feedback regarding how well you are learning skills—an essential ingredient in becoming a master of a skill. Third, they teach you methodologies, or practiced approaches, in applying their skills. Fourth, they empower you to think outside of the box. Finally, you build a relationship with your chief advocate. It is not always easy finding mentors, but it is worth seeking them out.

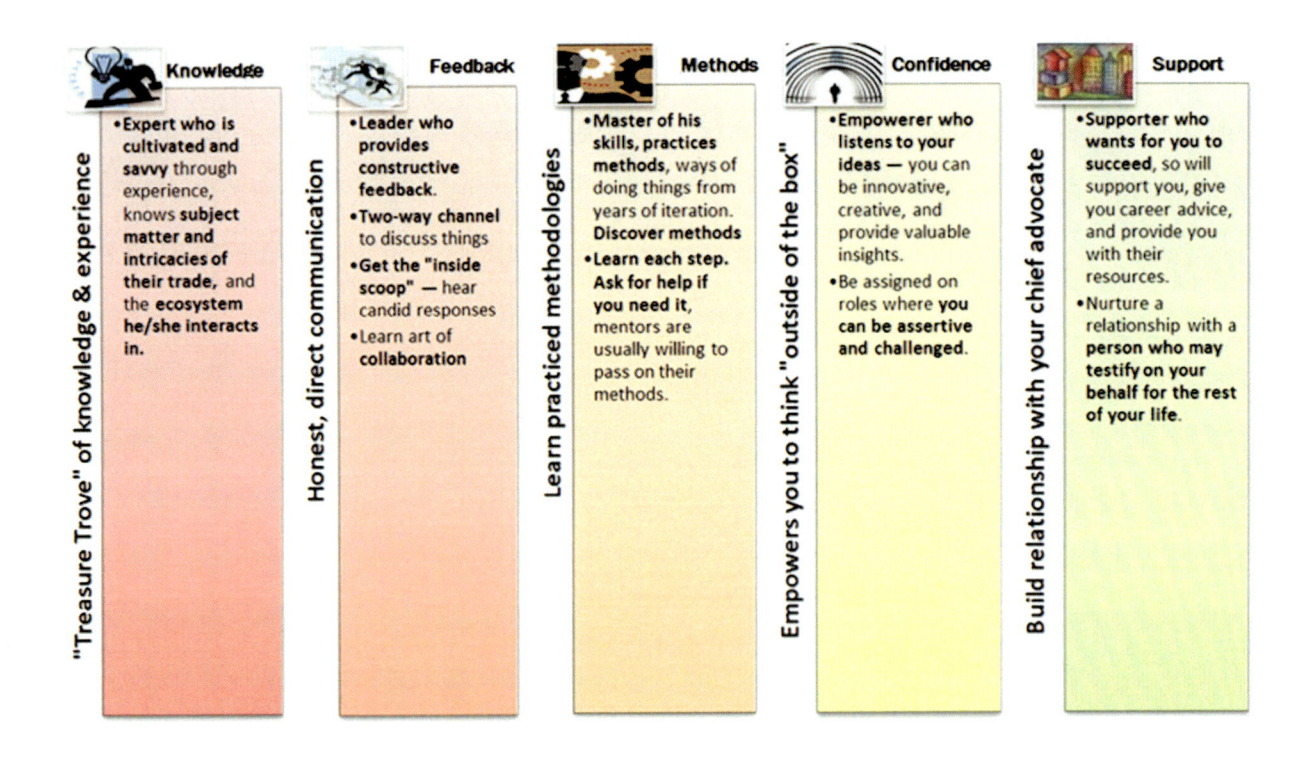

Knowledge	Feedback	Methods	Confidence	Support
•Expert who is cultivated and savvy through experience, knows subject matter and intricacies of their trade, and the ecosystem he/she interacts in.	•Leader who provides constructive feedback. •Two-way channel to discuss things •Get the "inside scoop" — hear candid responses •Learn art of collaboration	•Master of his skills, practices methods, ways of doing things from years of iteration. Discover methods •Learn each step. Ask for help if you need it, mentors are usually willing to pass on their methods.	•Empowerer who listens to your ideas — you can be innovative, creative, and provide valuable insights. •Be assigned on roles where you can be assertive and challenged.	•Supporter who wants for you to succeed, so will support you, give you career advice, and provide you with their resources. •Nurture a relationship with a person who may testify on your behalf for the rest of your life.
"Treasure Trove" of knowledge & experience	Honest, direct communication	Learn practiced methodologies	Empowers you to think "outside of the box"	Build relationship with your chief advocate

A benefit in having a mentor that often is overlooked is the passing-on of methodologies, or ways of applying a skill. A mentor is typically an expert in their field, someone who has been practicing their skill set for many years. Whether they learned a method from someone else or developed the method themselves, they have a proven way of applying their skills and are usually willing to pass it on to you. Examples of methods might be a design for programming, a style of writing, or managing files. A mentor wants you to succeed, so they are more than willing to pass on their methodologies to you.

Learning Methodologies

There are ways to apply a skill using different methodologies. You might learn a methodology while taking a course in college, though they are usually theoretical and teach you the overarching principles. So the best ways to learn methodologies are through companies that use them in their everyday business. Having a mentor is even more effective because, through your interpersonal interactions, you learn the intricacies of its application. This is one reason why universities champion the use of internships in their curriculum.

Applying a single skill might require the use of multiple methodologies. For example, here is a table that illustrates the methods you might learn for the skill of web design; notice how the methods come from scattered sources: books, courses, work projects, and a mentor.

Method	Source
Object-Oriented Programming	Learn it from a course in college, and then apply it in the actual development of applications.
Nomenclature for Naming Variables	Learn it from a college course
Use of Functions, Procedures	Conceptualize in a course in college, and then learn more about it by viewing examples in programs and books.
Web Page Structure	Review the structure of other websites, and read a book about search engine optimization.
Applying Style	Learn the use of CSS hands-on and by reading a book.
Planning/Scoping the Website	Learn this methodology from a mentor, who was meticulous in his planning.

During the building stage, as you are learning and building an expertise with a skill, you should understand the intricacies in each methodology you practice. You might have to use a particular methodology because your employer requires it. Once you become an expert with a skill, however, you will have the opportunity to use other methodologies that you have practiced in your experiences.

Decisions

After you finish a project, or after a certain amount of time has elapsed, you consider your options in moving forward with the development your skill set. Assessments give you an indication of your aptitude in learning skills, so you then can make a decision on what actions to take based on these results. There are three basic decisions: dropping the skill from your skill set, figuring out other ways to learn the skill, and identifying ways to advance your expertise with the skill.

Learning a new skill is an investment and takes extreme commitment, so if you cannot learn a skill with your current actions, you should find other ways of learning it or drop it from your skill set. Perhaps a skill is part of your skill set because it is a passion; you may find other ways to learn the skill, but not as a career pursuit at this stage in your life. For example, you may want to develop the skill of writing and have taken courses in college to build the skill, but if your grades are poor, you must stop allocating expensive resources to learn writing. Start a blog in your leisure time to learn how to write.

If you are effectively learning a skill, you should consider what to do next to build an expertise with it. In a way, you are going back to the planning stage to think of your next move—once again, your career stage dictates an action. If you are taking a course, you might simply take the more advanced class in the series. Otherwise, research what options are available, and decide what works best for you and fits into your desired skill set.

Presenting Stage

After you have learned and started to build an expertise with skills in your skill set, you are ready to present them to potential employers, co-workers, peers, and clients; each of them benefits by knowing your functional capabilities. This is the presenting stage of a skills-based approach, where you share your level of expertise with the skills in your skill set by promoting your skills through web services, search engines, and your personal website.

A skill set can be referred to as your *rational value*, a functional representation of what you have learned through your experiences. One of the main benefits of presenting a skill set is that it is searchable on various platforms, both externally and internally: *externally* meaning the search is conducted from another platform, such as a Google search; and *internally* meaning the search is conducted from the same platform, such as a search on a personal website. In the presenting stage of a skills-based approach, there are five ways to present your skill set: tagging, listing, explaining, demonstrating, and summarizing.

Ways to Present a Skill

Tagging
Tag your skills to content related to them, making the content accessible in searches.

Explaining
Describe how you apply your skill set in your professional experiences (like on a resume).

Demonstrating
Provide a sample of your work, where you demonstrate the use of your skill set.

Listing
Share your skill set as a list, which includes your level of expertise and endorsements for each skill.

Summarizing
Create a summary statement (objective, mission, or elevator pitch). Be authentic, talk about your top skills.

Tagging is a popular way to make content searchable. It requires taking a block of content, such as a blog entry, and assigning tags to the content. The tags are two- to three-word phrases that are indexed and the content appears when someone searches the tagged phrase. Skills can be assigned in a similar fashion. Assigning skills to your professional experiences (on your website, for example) will bring up your professional experiences when someone searches the skill.

***Listing* refers to sharing your skill set in a list format**, where you can provide information regarding your expertise with the skill, such as your years of experience with the skill and references or endorsements. This is LinkedIn's current approach; they dedicate a separate section of a profile to skills and add another layer of sophistication by letting your connections endorse them. Viewing a list of skills is like viewing a snapshot of your professional background; someone can make an immediate first impression of your functional capabilities. A recruiter can instantly determine whether you have the basic credentials for an employment opportunity. Likewise a client or associate understands how you will make the biggest impact while working with them.

***Explaining* means to describe how you have applied your skill set in your employment and educational experiences** like the presentation on a traditional résumé. In your explanations, reference the skill whenever possible. Create a results-oriented succinct statement about your experience. Your one-liner might be the only statement someone remembers after viewing your online résumé, profile, or personal website.

***Demonstrating* a skill is usually the most effective way to present a skill,** and for some skills it is a requirement. For example, demonstrating the skill of graphic design is necessary so someone can evaluate your creativity in developing graphics. Demonstrating a skill is best accomplished by providing a sample of work, which usually can be captured in a file—image, audio, video, spreadsheet, presentation, or document—all of which can be ported easily to an online web service. Whenever possible provide a demonstration of your skills, and let your audience come to their own conclusions regarding your level of expertise with a skill set.

***Summarizing* refers to creating a statement that mentions your top skills.** This brief statement might be called your *mission statement* or *objective statement* or *elevator pitch*. The focus is on your top skills. You want to deliver an authentic message that discusses your functional value—a skill set of your core competencies.

Validating Stage

The final stage in a skills-based approach is the validation stage. This is where you find ways to establish credibility with the skills in your skill set. You are already telling an audience you have these skills; now you want to prove your expertise with them. There are several reasons you need to validate your skills. Interested parties want to verify that you can do what you say you can do. The way you demonstrate skills often "sets a bar" that can be used to compare your level of expertise with another professional. Sometimes validation is a requirement for your responsibilities, such as a CPA certification in accounting. Finally, validating through the use of an endorsement or reference can provide added context to your experiences. It is important to have a validation strategy in order to prove your skills as a professional.

Why Validate Your Skills?

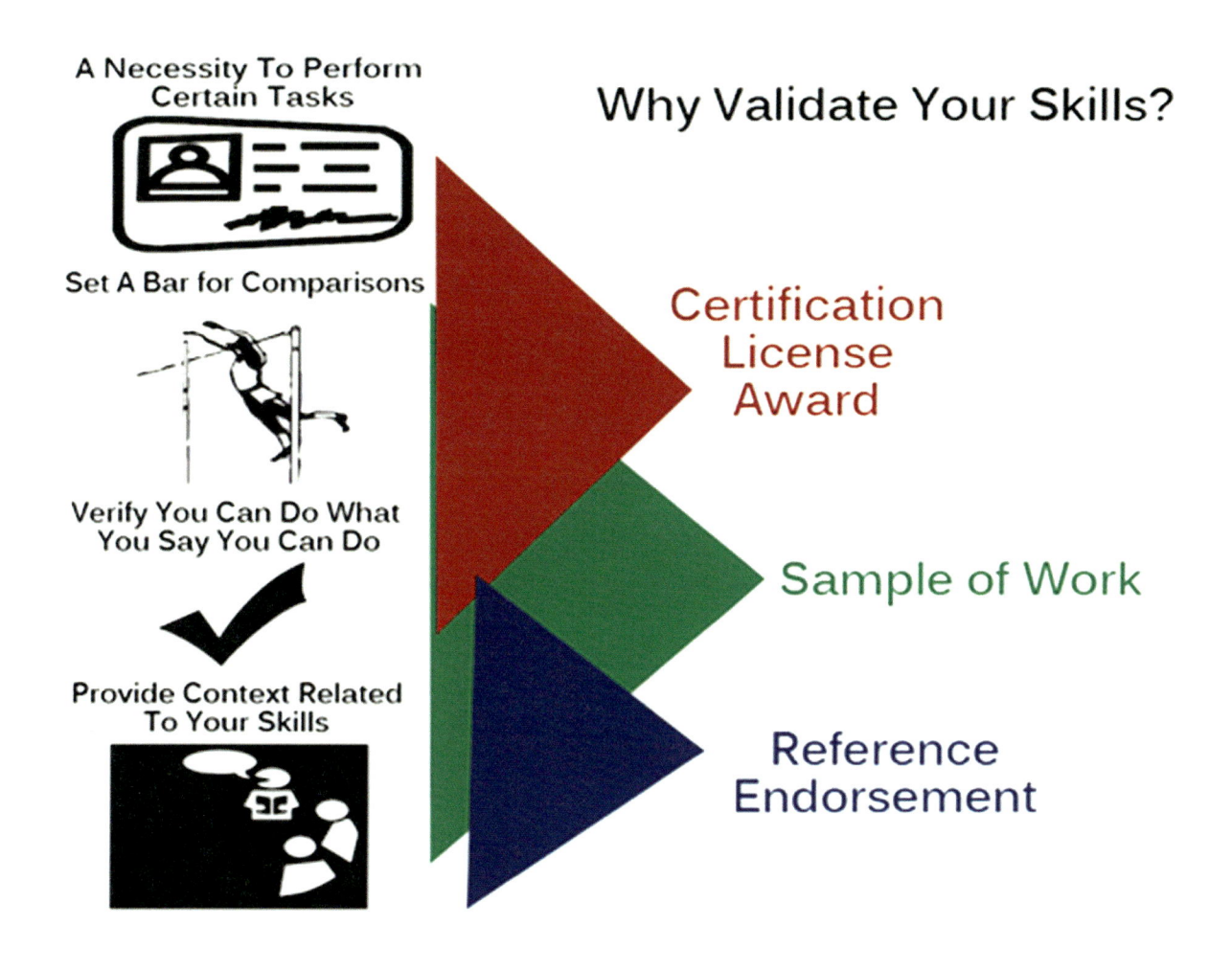

- A Necessity To Perform Certain Tasks
- Set A Bar for Comparisons
- Verify You Can Do What You Say You Can Do
- Provide Context Related To Your Skills

- Certification License Award
- Sample of Work
- Reference Endorsement

One reason to validate skills is to demonstrate accuracy in reporting your skills. As discussed earlier, it is extremely easy to apply to a job on a job board – it takes a click of a button. This means employers have to review many résumés without any prior screening. Employers have to digest résumés quickly by pinpointing skill sets and then validating each skill. They have to ensure you are accurately reporting your skill set, so be sure to validate your skill in order to move forward in the screening process.

Another reason for validating a skill set is to measure a skill level. Placement for some highly skilled professions is brutally competitive and requires exceeding a high bar that has been set. Top graduate school programs in business and law use the results of standardized tests as criteria in their admission decisions and will report a threshold of scores of their incoming class. This tells next year's applicant what score he or she will need to be accepted. There are a series of difficult accounting exams that are used to validate the skill level of top accountants.

Another reason for validating a skill set is to ensure basic knowledge of business practices. Financial analysts must pass certain tests to sell certain equities, accountants must pass a certification to perform certain duties, and lawyers have to pass a bar to practice law in a given state.

Another reason for validating a skill is to provide more context related to your experience in applying a skill. Someone can learn more about how you applied your skills when he or she reviews your skills. When you provide a work sample or a reference to validate skills, you also provide added context, a story or a demonstration of your work that makes you more memorable. Moreover, a reference has the opportunity to answer any questions that may have been raised about your skills.

There are a number of ways you can validate a skill. First, you can provide a work sample that demonstrates your skill expertise. Second, related to the first point, you can write and maintain a blog; this is a writing sample and shows you are keeping up with the most current ideas in your discipline. Third, you can provide a reference or endorsement who may be called on to elaborate about shared work experience; LinkedIn built a sophisticated interface based on this type of validation. Fourth, you can obtain a certification or award from a third party confirming your skill level. Finally, you can explain how you have applied a skill, and share how many years of experience you have with a skill.

Sample of Work

Provide a Sample of Work

Let a target audience draw their own conclusions regarding your level of expertise...

Portfolio

Graphics
Video
Links

Publications

Articles
Periodicals
Journals
Books

Coursework

Papers
Presentations
Projects

In most professional experiences, you create a work product that demonstrates your level of expertise with your skill set. If you have a sample of work that is a positive representation of your capabilities, find ways to publish it so that it is accessible to your target audience. A sample of work is an excellent way to validate skills because it lets your audience make their own unbiased evaluation. The biggest impediment in providing a sample of work is when you do not own or have copyright privilege to it. For example, you do the coding for a proprietary application while working for a previous employer, so you cannot share that application to demonstrate your programming capabilities. In this case, you rely on a reference and an explanation to validate your skills in building the application. There are many types of work samples, which will vary according to profession.

Students provide relevant coursework, such as papers, projects, and presentations. Because they lack employment experience, providing coursework samples is the best way to deliver content to potential employers. It is worth being selective by sharing only the best, most relevant pieces of work.

Writers and researchers provide writing samples. They should share their work, whether it is in published form or as an excerpt. Saying you have a writing skill needs to be validated by someone actually reading your work.

Web designers provide links to websites they created. A web designer must leave an impression of being tech savvy. Someone validating the skill of web design has to review a portfolio of websites.

Graphic designers provide a portfolio of their concepts. Graphic designers should share a portfolio of their creations; someone validating the skill of graphic design is going to want to evaluate creativity by seeing it firsthand.

If you are seeking employment, the most common venue to deliver a sample of work is during an interview. However, it is possible to share work samples on your personal website, so you should take advantage of this functionality. Why take the extra effort of going to an interview when the decision is going to be based on a sample of work? In addition, you provide content that you might not have been prompted to submit, and in most cases, it is better to provide as much content as possible. If you are not seeking employment, it is still worthwhile to share samples of your work. This establishes credibility with your ecosystem and the people and businesses with whom you interact. Providing other forms of media to supplement a textual profile significantly improves your first impression.

A Blog

Writing a blog is an excellent way to validate a skill set because it requires you to share insights. To write an effective blog, you commit to researching and understanding what is currently being published regarding the subject matter; in short, become an expert. Moreover, to add value, you think of ways to transform your message into something new and enlightening. Demonstrating that you can be creative and insightful is a powerful way to build credibility with a skill set.

Imagine two students who graduate with degrees in economics; one has a blog where he discusses what he has learned in his economic courses and makes interesting conclusions, and the other does not have a blog but has a marginally higher GPA. Who is going to get the job offer from an economic consulting firm? An employer leans toward the graduate with a blog because he can better predict his performance. The employer knows this candidate can conceptualize what he has learned and develop his own perspectives.

Mid-career professionals benefit from maintaining a blog because it requires them to keep on top of their field. To build a knowledge base, you need to feed on articles, other blogs, and books related to your field of expertise. Being insightful about your field demonstrates that you are becoming an expert.

Starting a blog is a challenging endeavor. You might not have developed the skill of writing. You might have periods of writer's block or be wary about publishing your thoughts to a target audience because you might feel ashamed if your writings are not well received. The best advice is to start writing a blog anyway. To start out, you might turn off the commenting function on the blog, or you might publish anonymously. You can decide later to publish under your name when you are ready. Blogging is an ongoing commitment, but you feel more confident with each time you publish a blog entry, and you will be inspired to prepare for the next one. Some of these ideas about writing a blog come from Seth Godin's book *The Icarus Deception*, where he argues we should become artists who produce valuable art—fresh, insightful work, and a blog can be art.

The main advantage in using a blog to validate your skill set is that your personality resonates through your perspectives; injecting emotional value into the presentation of your skill set can be refreshing—it shows you are human.

References/Endorsements

Providing references is an established practice when sending a resume. When you apply to a traditional job posting, you provide a list of references with their contact information, and it is understood that the hiring organization will probably call them. The concept of validating a skill with an endorsement has become popular with LinkedIn.

Once you build a skill set with your LinkedIn profile, your connections can endorse the skills through an interface where they are automatically prompted to do so. Your skills are shown in a ranked list depending on the number of endorsements related to a skill. It is worth making sure your best advocates are endorsing your skills, so they will be contacted to testify on your behalf. It is also worth keeping your skills list up-to-date with your LinkedIn profile, so you can take advantage of the network effect of social media to validate your skill set.

The biggest advantage in using a reference is that they can "tell a story" about their experiences with you. Providing the added context can make it easier for someone to understand your contribution. Moreover, by answering a probe about an experience, a reference addresses exactly what has spurred someone's intrigue; it might be your only opportunity to provide a response to their questions. Communicating with endorsements and references has become much easier; you simply send an e-mail, and the reference can respond whenever they get the opportunity. There is no haggling over when to make a phone call. Social media has facilitated the process of making connections, establishing references, and having your skills validatated by a reference.

Why Use a Reference

A reference...

Tells a Story
Back in 2010 we worked together on this project... I remember when we launched the application, our client flew in from Japan, and we had a conference...

Has a Reputation
I have 10 years of experience developing applications and...

Shares Details
The MS Access application was built in 6 months...

Provides Context
I designed the application and he programmed it. The application was built to improve the profitability of our client...

Makes an Evaluation
His programming skills are better than average...

Certifications/Awards/Licenses

Obtaining a certification has become more common in most professions, particularly in information technology, where there are rapid changes in the adoption of applications, technologies, and languages. The advantage of a certification is bringing in a third party to objectively validate an expertise with a skill. Using certifications has a few benefits. First, becoming certified is a way to evaluate how well a professional has learned a skill when he or she had to learn it quickly (such as learning a new technology). For example, you might learn to develop websites in one programming language and then have to switch to another one, like a transition from ASP Classic to ASP.Net. You learn the new language from a book, so you want to become certified to demonstrate your proficiency. Second, some professions demand a high degree of skill and require a certification to "set the bar"—lawyers must pass a bar exam in their state to practice law. Third, it can be used to demonstrate understanding of the ethics required in a profession; financial analysts must pass a series of tests before they can sell and distribute certain equities. Finally, a certification can be used for personal branding—presenting a badge makes a great first impression.

It is worth discovering what certifications are available for your skill set and whether they are a requirement for your targeted careers. Many professions have an umbrella organization that manages information about them, and you can learn about certifications through their websites. For example, an accountant can learn more about the CPA exam by visiting the website of American Institute of Certified Public Accountants. If you cannot find a representative organization, you can utilize a search service such as CareerOneStop, sponsored by the US Department of Labor, to find available certifications.

Certifications might have a prerequisite, such as taking a course, and usually require a significant time and/or financial investment, so it is worth investigating everything upfront. You should conduct a cost-versus-benefit analysis, and assess your capabilities in completing the certification before making any commitment.

Once you get certified, you will want to brandish a badge. The concept of a badge is to present and validate a skill with a simple graphic that is verified by a third party. It is meant to function similar to a SSL certificate, where a website is verified to be secure. Badges are an excellent way to brand an expertise with a skill set.

Badge Concept

There is a movement for the adoption of digital badges, which demonstrate a proficiency and/or level of expertise with skills. Badges are designed to present a more precise indication of a skill level than a college degree and do not require the huge financial investment of a college degree. This is why Mozilla, an organization leading the development of digital badge systems, is actively meeting with providers of free online courses (MOOCs). A badge is an image with information about the achievement. For example, a badge might include information about when it was issued, background information about the organization providing the badge, and the score a professional earned on a test.[28]

Badge Concept for Validating a Skill

Beginner
ASP .Net
3 years of experience
Passed Level I Certification
Verified By Microsoft

Intermediate
SQL Language
6 years of experience
Passed Level II Certification
Verified By Oracle

Expert
MS Excel
6 years of experience

Verified By Self

Basic Information:

How many years of experience, when the skill was last used, and the definition of the skill.

Verification Information:

When and how a person became certified.

Information about the rubrics - a standardized assessment test - used to become certified. Other information such as a test score, professsor, etc.

Native Platform
Personal Website, Social Media Profile, Online Resume, etc.

Organization Issuing the Badge
Microsoft, Oracle, WW3 etc.,

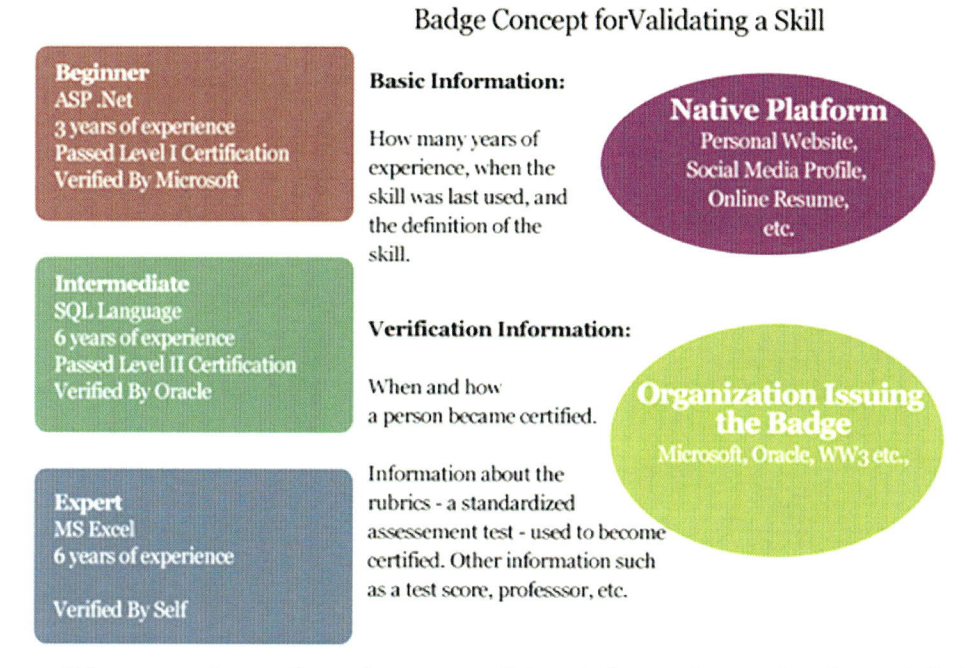

Digital badges will become the preferred way to validate information technology skills because the type of professionals who use them feed on competition, and technologies move too fast to be captured with college degrees. For example, if you are a self-taught teenage programmer, why invest in a college degree in computer science when you can compete and earn a digital badge?

Validation Strategy

Putting together a validation strategy might be the best way to establish credibility with your ecosystem. There are three items to cover in a validation strategy: make sure each skill in your skill set is validated, employ the best possible validation techniques, and make sure your top skills are highlighted. The first step is to draw a diagram with lines connecting skills to the techniques used the validate them. Does each skill have at least one connection? The second step is to put yourself in the frame of mind of someone from your target audience, and draw conclusions about your credibility after viewing your skill set on a given platform. Are you assured and confident about your skill set? Make sure you are properly validating your skill set by employing a validating strategy.

Actionable

The skills-based approach is a methodology that every professional should practice. It organizes the complexities of planning and developing a career into four simple stages: planning, building, presenting, and validating. Within each stage, there are concrete and actionable methods to employ to achieve the intended result of developing a skill set. In suggesting a framework you might actually follow, it must be accessible, actionable, not too tedious, and enjoyable; otherwise you might read and understand the concepts but never do it. The skills-based approach has these characteristics.

There are many books that guide you through a methodology and provide a table to pencil in your ideas. Most of the concepts of a skills-based approach are already integrated in professional web services, so you manage your skill set on the different platforms you utilize: a personal website, LinkedIn profile, and/or MonsterJobs profile.

Sometimes books or web services present a methodology that makes sense but does not explain how to use it in your everyday life. The skills-based approach lays out a sequential path in developing a skill set and suggests specific, concrete actions at each stage.

When you introduce something new to your life, you do not want to add something that is time-consuming. Filling out long forms or paperwork can be bothersome. You can manage your skill set from an MS Excel worksheet, however, as you progress through the development of a skills-based approach. (Downloadable sample templates are available at www.skillsbasedapproach.com.) Some of the suggested actions, such as taking a personality test, might seem tedious, but you can always find other ways to get the same results. The general premise of planning and tracking the development of no more than fifteen skills in your skill set should not be overbearing, however.

Thinking about what you want to accomplish in your career can be enlightening and exciting. Planning exactly what you want to commit to and the contribution you want to leave behind is very inspiring. The development of a skill set is a framework to help you formulate a plan to reach your career aspirations, so it should be enjoyable.

Conclusions

Part of Your Personal Online Brand

A skill set represents your rational value—your functional capabilities, or what you bring to the table. It is one component of your personal brand. The complement to your skill set is your aura, which represents your emotional value—your human value, charisma, and presence. The other component is your identity, which represents your connections and how you are represented in networks. Altogether, these three components represent your online personal brand.

Representing and developing your functional capabilities is very important, but it is also important to develop your human capabilities. First impressions and the quality of your relationships have a major effect on your career because if you do not generate intrigue, you might not ever have the interactions you need to become successful. Moreover, there should be a strong linkage between your skill set and your aura so that you are presenting your authentic self.[29]

A skills-based approach is ideal for career planning and development, and skills are an effective representation of your rational value. As more professional web services adopt skill sets, there will be improvements in functionality: searching on skill sets, presenting skills, validating skills as badges, and interactivity between platforms. However, skill sets are just one component of an online personal brand, and the development of your aura and identity also play an important role in your success as a professional. A personal website acts as the centerpiece of your online personal brand.

A Simple Solution

The basic premise of a skills-based approach is to concentrate on developing a skill set as you navigate through your career. A skills-based approach relieves some of the pressure we face with career planning and development, including fluctuating career demands due to the rapid adoption of new technologies, skyrocketing education costs, a tightening employment market, and underemployment.

Our economy is in transition from an Industrial Age to an Information Age. Technology is being embraced by every sector of our economy, which means most professionals must learn new technologies. This is usually a multi-step process that is much better summarized with skills. First you learn transferable skills, such as computational thinking and problem solving, and then technical skills, such as website analytics. With our current education system, you most likely learn these skills while earning a college degree. Then you leverage your experience with transferable and technical skills while being trained to use specific software and/or hardware in the workplace. One reason why you learn a specific technology after you get a college degree is because of the speed new technologies are adopted; it happens too fast for a planned curriculum or even an online book. The primary value of a college degree is the collection of transferable and technical skills you learn. A skills-based approach suggests tracking the development of your skills and understanding transferable skills, so you are equipped to handle changes in technologies. Dan Schawbel says, "By focusing on delivering results, being remarkable, learning new skills to adapt to our ever-changing world, you can make your brand memorable, and opportunities for success will follow."[30]

Rising education costs are making the average professional rethink the value of a college degree (or at least the most cost-effective way to earn one); the average cost of public and private schools nearly doubled between 2001 and 2011.[31] The value of a college degree is going to be heavily scrutinized, especially the first couple of years when students take core classes where they learn transferable skills that are not necessarily related to their career pursuits. It may be beneficial to acquire transferable skills through a community college instead of an expensive university. Is there a discernible difference between taking a calculus course at different universities or a community college? Moreover, with the introduction of free online courses, professors from top universities like Harvard, MIT, and Berkeley are giving the lectures. A skills-based approach provides leeway so you can be more precise, thrifty, and efficient as you learn skills.

The employment market is increasingly competitive. Part of the problem is that students graduate with degrees tailored for particular careers even though the demand for them is saturated. For example, law schools have started to decrease their incoming class sizes because it is difficult to place their graduates. A solution to this dilemma is to plan your career based on transferable skills, which can be utilized across subjects and disciplines. This allows flexibility in the case you decide to change careers. In addition, since the future demand for skills is published, you plan to build a skill set that will be in high demand and therefore increase the likelihood of finding an opportunity when you are ready. For career planning, predicting the demand for skills might be more effective than predicting the demand for careers.

Underemployment is when skilled workers have jobs that do not require their level of education.[32] For example, someone who recently graduated with a degree in marketing works in a coffee shop making a little more than minimum wage because there are few other opportunities specifically looking for "marketers". Using a skills-based approach alleviates the problem of underemployment. First, you define your professional experience and knowledge as a skill set rather than as a degree, so you are more flexible to adapt to the current job market. You should have a choice of career paths to choose from based on your skill set. Second, you find ways to make any job an opportunity to develop your skills; your job becomes a stepping-stone to something in the future. Though you are a cashier at a coffee shop, you can volunteer to create a website for the coffee shop to develop your skills of website design and marketing promotions. Third, you can build your skills on your own time to land a long-term career. You may choose to volunteer, take an online course, or read a book to advance your expertise with skills. Whatever you choose, you become more marketable for future opportunities. Building skills is more efficient and accessible and costs less than earning another degree.

Moving Forward

Skills sets are currently being utilized in many web services. However, the value of a skills-based approach could be improved with the implementation of a few steps.

(1) Course listings at university and colleges should explicitly mention what skills are being learned. It makes sense that when you take a course, you know precisely what skills you are going to learn. This is especially important when you are learning transferable skills, such as writing and research (learned through a humanities class) or computational thinking (learned through a computer science class). The cost of education is increasing rapidly, so students should efficiently plan every course to develop a skill in their desired skill set.

(2) Colleges should teach transferable skills that can be utilized across disciplines. As students make the transition to professionals, they need be prepared by having a skill set that allows for them to react to rapid changes in technology and demographics – two characteristics of the modern-age.

(3) There should be a universal list of skills with definitions. Professionals need a commonly understood list of skills to understand the meaning of a skill and any nuances between one skill and another. For example, it is currently hard to differentiate between the skills of website design and website development. A universal list of skills also makes sense for recruiters searching on skills; they need to be confident that their search results encompass the right pool of candidates.

(4) Providers of skills lists need to agree to a universal method of assigning skills. There are two barriers with the current implementations of assigning skills. First, there is no clear way to handle specific technologies. For example, in LinkedIn you list HTML as a skill, but in other platforms, the skill is web design and HTML is a programming language. Second, there should be delineation between assigning *transferable skills* and *technical skills*.

(5) The demand for skills should be tracked. Rapid changes in technology and demographics are affecting the responsibilities for different careers. Professionals have to adapt and retool their skill sets to accommodate these changes. Therefore, it makes sense to publish the future demand for skills. Professionals can better anticipate and plan to build an expertise with skills needed for their career. They can also target developing a skill set that will be in high demand and increase their chances of landing an opportunity.

(6) Skills sets should be portable from one platform to another. Currently, it is a requirement to maintain a skill set on different platforms because each of them is proprietary. The main disadvantage is redundancy and inefficiency. It would be ideal to be able build one skill set list that can be used effectively across platforms. For example, Mozilla created the concept of a backpack - a collection of online badges - that can be referenced across various platforms.

Appendix: Application of Methodology

Website Developer Career

To demonstrate the application of a skills-based approach, this appendix depicts how three individuals in different professions and stages in their life utilize the methodology to plan and develop their careers. These individuals are fictitious, though much of the information is drawn from actual experiences and assessments. Each example has a brief synopsis of the individual. This is followed by the implementation of a skills-based approach displayed in tables at the different stages: the planning and building stage for all three examples, and validating stage for the first example (due to the individual being a mid-career professional). All of these tables are downloadable as blank templates from www.skillsbasedapproach.com.

Biography

John is a mid-career professional. He develops websites for small businesses. Like many web developers he is always thinking of the next great idea. He received a degree in Business. His website design skills were learned through his employment experiences.

Planning Stage

	Personality Test	Interests Test	
	Overall	*Primary*	*Secondary*
Self-Awareness	INTJ Introvert, Intuitive, Thinker, Judger	Enterprising	Conventional
	Takeaways	I am self-motivated and enjoy the challenge of being insightful. I am a thinker and want to be part of the decision making process. My interests indicate that I am adventurous and competitive, and like to have everything orderly.	
Passion Theory	Early in college, I developed a strong passion for writing because I enjoy communicating ideas; though writing does not come easy to me. I am passionate about actualizing new ideas.		
Craftsman Mindset	Throughout my employment experiences, I have repeatedly demonstrated a strong aptitude in designing and creating database and website applications.		

Product to Market	Product Differentiation	Target Market	Value Proposition
	Designing website and database applications, communicating technical ideas effectively.	I work with web developers, graphic designers, entrepreneurs, social marketers, and career counselors.	I have strong business acumen to compliment technical skills in developing database and website applications. I bridge the communication gap between IT and business professionals.

An Action Plan

My Skill Set	Sub Skills	Actions
Technical Skills		
Website Development	ASP .NET 4.0, Jquery, AJAX, HTML5, SQL	Prepare for ASP .Net certification.
Database Design	SQL Server, MS Access	Take an online course to familiarize myself with enterprise database systems.
Graphic Design	Adobe Photoshop	Take lead role in developing graphics on website projects. Use Adobe Photoshop whenever possible. Learn effective methods for layering.
Application Development		Have experience with this skill, but do not plan to develop it at this point.
Business Management		Take seminars to identify resources in the community that support managing a business and understanding key responsibilities.
Professional Business Writing		Read books, articles, blogs, and forums to learn best practices of writers.
Traditional Transferable Skills		
Leadership Skills		Research techniques of visionary leaders.
Communication Skills		Practice verbal skills by teaching a course in the community. Learn best practices for communicating in social media.
Emerging Transferable Skills		
Transdiscipinarity		Continue understanding the disciplines related to a personal website service, such as career development and website development.
New-Media Literacy		Cloud computing has become a widely accepted platform to deliver new services. Attend seminars and perhaps take a course on cloud computing.

Building Stage

My Skill Set	Sub Skills				
Technical Skills		**Assessment**	**Mentor**	**Methodologies**	**Next Step**
Website Development	ASP .NET 4.0, Jquery, AJAX, HTML5, SQL	Finished an online preparation course for ASP .Net certification. Scored well on the practice test, and signed up to take a certification test.		While taking the preparation course, learned a faster way to code using Razor syntax.	Take the certification exam.
Database Design	SQL Server, MS Access	Completed course on large, enterprise databases. Learned key concepts, however, have not applied them.		Learned how to plan and build a large database with over 1,000,000 transactions an hour.	Take on a project to create an enterprise database.
Graphic Design	Adobe Photoshop	My peers gave mixed reviews regarding my graphic design work.		Continuing learning about layers.	Take on new graphic design work.
Business Management		In a seminar class for startups, learned how to make connections with investors, universities, and leaders. Made 100 new connections.	An instructor shared candid insights and connections with me.		Continue making connections and attend more seminars.
Professional Business Writing		Received positive feedback from my target audience with my blogs and articles.			Continue improving on composition and paragraph structure.
Traditional Transferable Skills					
Communication Skills		Taught a class and had a good reception; many of the attendees signed up for another class.			Work on telling stories in presentations. Stories are more memorable.
Emerging Transferable Skills					

Transdiscipinarity		Read books from experts in career planning and development. Conceptualizing how to apply the concepts in a personal website service.			Translate what I learned about career planning and development into something actionable online.
New-Media Literacy		Watched seminar on cloud computing and have a better understanding of its advantages and disadvantages.			Learn how to use cloud computing.

Validation Stage

My Skill Set	Sub Skills	Work Sample	Reference	Certification	Other
Technical Skills					
Website Development	ASP .NET 4.0, Jquery, AJAX, HTML5, SQL	On my personal website, provide a portfolio of websites.	On my personal website, provide references. On LinkedIn, use endorsements for website development skills.	Signing up to take a Microsoft certification class.	
Database Design	SQL Server, MS Access		References validate usability in managing content on their website.	Become certified with MS SQL Server.	
Graphic Design	Adobe Photoshop	On my personal website, highlight websites where I did the graphics.			
Business Management		On my personal website, share coursework from MBA.	In LinkedIn, have connections endorse this skill.		
Professional Business Writing		Publish articles in social media, and on my personal website.			Maintain blog about ideas in career planning and development.
Traditional Transferable skills					
Communication Skills		Provide videos of presentations and classes.			
Emerging Transferable skills					
Transdiscipinarity					Write blog that discusses career planning and development through the lens of projecting an online personal brand.

Salesman Career

Biography

Mary is an early career professional and *passively seeking* other opportunities. She sells information technology services for a small company, but feels she has potential to do more. She received an undergraduate degree in economics from a reputable public university.

Planning Stage

	Personality Test	**Interests Test**	
	Overall	*Primary*	*Secondary*
Self-Awareness	**ENFP** Extrovert, Intuitive, Feeler, Perceivers	Enterprising	Social
	Takeaway	I enjoy being around others. I am compassionate and a listener. I am cool headed when I work. My interests indicate that I am ambitious, yet want to be around others.	
Passion Theory	I do not have this *lifelong career passion*. In college, I built amazing relationships while I was in a sorority; I earned a degree in economics and received average grades. I passionately argue my side in a debate on politics or economics, sometimes my ability to be insightful is overlooked.		
Craftsman Mindset	In a few experiences, I demonstrated being extremely level-headed during highly stressful situations. I have a way of reassuring those around me.		
Product to Market	**Product Differentiation**	**Target Market**	**Value Proposition**
	Crisis management, team building, customer service	Small to medium sized businesses in northern California looking for a sales representative or a management team looking for a team player	I have insightful ideas and work well with others. I am a good fit as part of a management team, where I am not necessarily the leader, but the glue that brings everyone together.
An Action Plan			
My Skill Set	**Sub Skills**	**Actions**	
Technical Skills			
IT Sales		Attend on-site training for delivering sales pitches and closing deals.	

Sales Forecasting	Salesforce and Zoho CRM	Learn strategies for planning and forecasting sales.
Sales Networking	Hootesuite and IContact	Build a presence on Twitter and LinkedIn. Learn how to use groups, forums, and blogs to connect with potential clients.
Economics		A skill learned in college but do not plan to continue developing at this point.
Project Management	Clarizen	A skill to develop in the long-term. Take an online course to learn fundamentals and/or seek an entry-level position to learn best practices.
Team Building		A skill that comes naturally to me according to the results of a self-awareness test. Volunteer for a local organization to be part of a team.
Traditional Transferable skills		
Verbal Communication		Join a local Toastmasters chapter to practice presenting and connecting with others.
Emerging Transferable skills		
Social Intelligence		Making deep connections is a strength of mine, so should commit to building this skill.
Virtual Collaboration	Skype, Twitter	A project management position requires learning to communicate with a team virtually. For now, commit to developing lasting connections in LinkedIn.

Building Stage

My Skill Set	Sub Skills				
Technical Skills		**Assessment**	**Mentor**	**Methodologies**	**Next Step**
IT Sales		Attended two seminars to learn better techniques for selling IT software. Month to month sales increased 20% - an anchor to my self-assessment.	My direct supervisor is a huge asset. He has taught me to be confident in persuading potential clients.	Learned a method for starting connections; incremental gift giving.	Work with my supervisor to learn more of his methods. Keep attending new seminars.

Sales Networking		My goal was to establish a foothold in Twitter and LinkedIn. Added twenty LinkedIn connections and fifty Twitter followers.		To make Twitter and LinkedIn connections learned a method of give and take.	Start a simple blog.
Project Management		Have not had time to take an online course.			Plan to take an online course in the future.
Team Building		Coached youth softball team. Learning how girls interact on a team.			Continue coaching and finding ways to create a *competitive spark*.
Emerging Transferable skills					
Social Intelligence		Become a motivator at work (like my supervisor).			Discuss with my supervisor his techniques to motivate us.
Virtual Collaboration		Realize that I will never meet many of my connections face-to-face.			

Teacher Career

Biography

Karen is a student in her third year at a regional college, where she is working towards a degree in elementary education. In the short-term, she is trying to finish her teaching assessments and placements while getting good grades. In the long-term, she wants to be an elementary school teacher in the same area where she was raised and her family currently resides. She believes landing a teaching position will be especially difficult because she has narrowed her focus to a particular area.

Planning Stage

	Personality Test	Interests Test	
	Overall	*Primary*	*Secondary*
Self-Awareness	ESFJ Extrovert, Sensor, Feeler, Judger	Social	Realistic
	Takeaway	I make strong bonds and meeting new people comes natural to me. I demonstrate patience and compassion while working with others. My interests indicate that I like to nurture relationships, by teaching or caring for others. I am straightforward and make sure everything is grounded.	
Passion Theory	Teaching has always been my career pursuit. I enjoy teaching something to someone and seeing their face light up when they get it. I love softball so I might coach.		
Craftsman Mindset	Throughout my life, I have demonstrated a capacity to make strong personal bonds with others. After I make a first impression, the person remembers me and wants to maintain a connection. Children seem to gravitate to me.		
Product to Market	Product Differentiation	Target Market	Value Proposition
	Strong interpersonal, verbal, and teaching skills, understand the developmental needs of children	Elementary schools in Waterloo (where my family lives); upstate New York elementary schools.	I have a unique talent in identifying the needs of children. I understand how to communicate and educate children to maximize their learning potential.
Action Plan			
My Skill Set	Sub Skills	Actions	
Technical Skills			
Elementary Education		Finish taking classes and placements to graduate. Apply to Master's programs at colleges located near my hometown.	

Classroom Management		Begin to familiarize myself with this skill during my first few placements.
Classroom Assessment		Take a course on assessing the learning capabilities of young children.
Parent Teacher Communication		Take a course on this form of communication. Hope to have the opportunity to practice speaking or writing to parents during my placements, otherwise I will have to wait until my first placement.
Guided Reading		Take a course on teaching children to read.
Traditional Skills		
Planning/Organizing		Take a course on developing lesson plans. Self-commit to following a to-do list and schedule to organize my day.
Communication Skills		Take courses to keep reading, writing, and verbal skills sharp.

Building Stage

My Skill Set	Sub Skills				
Technical Skills		**Assessment**	**Mentor**	**Methodologies**	**Next Step**
Elementary Education		Finished semester with excellent grades in courses related to elementary education. Had positive feedback from the teacher I worked with in my internship placement.	The teacher during my placement passed along helpful advice in interacting with eager children.	Learned simple grading techniques to reinforce positive behavior.	Finish my senior year of courses and another internship placement.
Classroom Management		Challenging spreading my attention to 30 students, but by the end of the placement, it was more comfortable.		Learned simple facial cues to keep children engaged.	Have another internship placement during my senior year. Hope to start with the same confidence I left this one with.
Classroom Assessment		Took course on classroom assessments and it was informative, but somewhat theoretical.			Hope to practice this skill in my next placement.
Parent-Teacher Communication		Witnessed a lot of parent involvement with their children during my placement.			Assert myself to communicate with parents in my next placement (if possible).

Appendix: Transferable skills

Some skills are transferable across disciplines and subject matter. For example, say you are good writer, an employer may hire you to write a user manual for an application even though you have no prior experience with the application; they figure to train you with the application and then leverage your skill in writing. So *transferable skills* are a basic foundation, something employers build upon as they teach the intricacies of their business.

Traditional Transferable Skills

Traditional transferable skills are ones that are already utilized by our workforce today. In many cases, these skills become your foundation as you learn more sophisticated technical skills.

Traditional (Transferable) Skills Most Sought After By Employers[33]	
Communication Skills	Listening, verbal, and written.
Analytic/Research Skills	Assess a situation, understanding varying perspectives, and gathering data.
Computer/Technical Literacy	Understand basic hardware and software, email, social media, and networking.
Flexibility/Adaptability/Managing Multiple Projects	Multi-tasking.
Interpersonal Abilities	Ability to relate to co-workers, clients, and colleagues.
Leadership/Management Skills	Take charge and manage co-workers.
Planning/Organizing	Ability to design, plan, organize, and implement projects and tasks.
Problem Solving/Reasoning/Creativity	Find solutions to problems using your creativity, reasoning, and past experiences.
Teamwork	Ability to work with others

Emerging Transferable Skills

Emerging transferable skills are ones that will be in high demand in the near future. A team from *Institute For The Future* released a well-conceived study to identify them. They used six drivers of change: extreme longevity, rise of smart machines and systems, computational world, new media ecology, super structured organizations, and globally connected world; there is a detailed discussion about each of these drivers in their study. The skills and their definitions are in the table below.

Emerging Transferable Skills[34]	
Sense-Making	Ability to determine the deeper meaning or significance of what is being expressed.
Social Intelligence	Ability to connect to others in a deep and direct way, to sense and stimulate reactions and desired interactions.
Novel & Adaptive Thinking	Proficiency at thinking and coming up with solutions and responses beyond that which is rote or rule-based.
Cross-Cultural Competency	Ability to operate in different cultural settings.
Computational Thinking	Ability to translate vast amounts of data into abstract concepts and to understand data-based reasoning.
New-Media Literacy	Ability to critically assess and develop content that uses new media forms, and to leverage these media for persuasive communication.
Transdisciplinarity	Literacy in and ability to understand concepts across multiple disciplines.
Design Mindset	Ability to represent and develop tasks and work processes for desired outcomes.
Cognitive Load Management	Ability to discriminate and filter information for importance, and to understand how to maximize cognitive functioning using a variety of tools and techniques.
Virtual Collaboration	Ability to work productively, drive engagement, and demonstrate presence as a member of a virtual team.

Soft Skills

In the book Emotional Intelligence 2.0, Travis Bradberry and Jean Greaves define emotional intelligence and provide strategies to improve your score – something they argue will improve work performance not matter what your profession. They list soft skills related to emotional intelligence.[35]

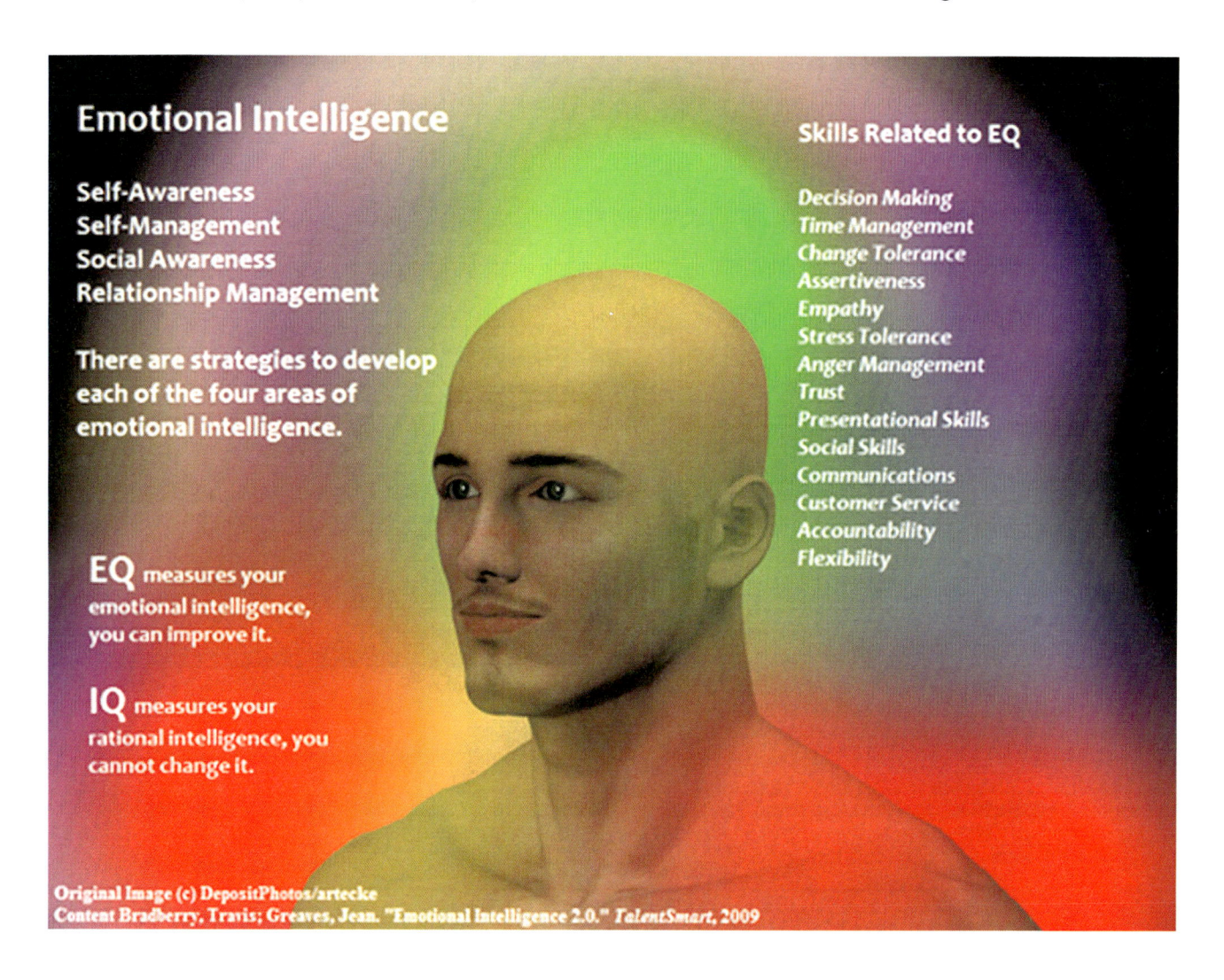

Emotional Intelligence

Self-Awareness
Self-Management
Social Awareness
Relationship Management

There are strategies to develop each of the four areas of emotional intelligence.

EQ measures your emotional intelligence, you can improve it.

IQ measures your rational intelligence, you cannot change it.

Skills Related to EQ

Decision Making
Time Management
Change Tolerance
Assertiveness
Empathy
Stress Tolerance
Anger Management
Trust
Presentational Skills
Social Skills
Communications
Customer Service
Accountability
Flexibility

Original Image (c) DepositPhotos/artecke
Content Bradberry, Travis; Greaves, Jean. "Emotional Intelligence 2.0." *TalentSmart*, 2009

Appendix: Mozilla Universal Badges

Since early 2011, Mozilla has spearheaded a project to develop the technology and infrastructure for universally accepted online badges. The framework for these online badges includes: the badge itself (an image and textual content), an assessment, and infrastructure. An important aspect of this infrastructure is a mechanism where a third-party verifies badges they issue; for now, it is a combination of attached metadata and a hyperlink back to the provider.[36] These online badges make validating skills much easier because it ensures every skill can be validated and ported across different platforms (such as personal and company websites, social media profiles, and blog platforms). Moreover, as institutions embrace these online badges, they become more credible – making an impact in employment decisions and school acceptances. Finally, it enables independent organizations to issue online badges based on their own *rubrics* – a standard of performance for defined population. This significantly expands the number of possible learning channels.

Benefits Of Mozilla's Universal Online Badges
Effectively complements skills (an excellent way to validate skills). It is possible to apply a one-to-one or many-to-one relationship between skills and online badges.
Provides more context. For example, an online badge shares more information than simply a grade after completing a course.
Evolves to capture changes in technology, education, and skills.
Accepted and functional across various professional and personal web services.
Relationship builder for communities.
Useful as a self-assessment while building skills.
Establishes a linkage and acceptance between formal and informal leaning. Creates a much wider spectrum of learning channels.

As you use online badges to validate your skills, there are two things to consider. First, use ones that serve a purpose and do not add unnecessary clutter – concentrate on the quality, not the quantity of online badges you acquire. Second, check out the provider of the badge and think about their use of rubrics to assess your skill level. It is an open system so any organization can provide badges; there is nothing akin to the accreditation process colleges go through to establish credibility.

Appendix: Survey

A survey was conducted in December 2012 to understand the effectiveness of some basic premises of the skills-based approach methodology. The objective was to answer three primary questions. Are recruiters searching for candidates based on their skill set? What should be key drivers in career planning based on skills? What are effective ways to build and validate skills? The purpose of the survey was not necessarily to make definitive conclusions based on statistical significance, but rather capture prevailing thoughts.

SurveyMonkey, an established web service for conducting surveys, was utilized to disseminate the survey and collect all responses. The survey was delivered to one hundred nineteen persons who identify themselves as human resource professionals. This designation was chosen because the responsibilities of this type of professional might include recruiting to fill employment positions, conducting employment evaluations, and participating in training employees. Moreover, human resource professionals interact with employees on a personal level so might better understand their motivations and learning experiences.

Here are some conclusions from the survey:

- The best way to build a skill is to take on a project at work – eighty seven percent of the respondents reported it as very effective.
- Most of the respondents (sixty-nine percent) have searched on a skill set.
- Reviewing a sample of work is the best way to validate a skill.
- The clear majority of the respondents strongly agree that you can learn a skill if you work on developing it and are determined to learn it properly.

Here is information about the sample:

- 119 Human Resource professionals, all from the United States

- 82.7% of the respondents are over 30 years old and the largest segment (41.8%) is between 45 and 60.

- 60.9% of the respondents are women

- 65.4% have a college degree

- Over 20 different industries and services are represented

- There were 9 respondents who did not report their demographic information

I can learn a skill if I work on developing it and am determined to learn it properly.

Disagree		Agree Somewhat		Strongly Agree
○	○	○	○	○

Other (please specify)
[   ]

I should only develop skills based on my strengths.

Disagree		Somewhat Agree		Strongly Agree
○	○	○	○	○

Other (please specify)
[   ]

I should pursue a career and develop skills based on the results of a personality test.

Disagree		Somewhat Agree		Strongly Agree
○	○	○	○	○

Other (please specify)
[   ]

What is the best way to validate a skill (1 being the most important)?

- [▾] reference who describes their experiences with you
- [▾] a certificate from a third-party
- [▾] sample of work (coursework, publications, etc.)
- [▾] years of experience

What is a better indication of someone's level of expertise with a skill?

Years of Experience		Neutral		Application of Skill
○	○	○	○	○

Other (please specify)
[   ]

Have you ever searched for a candidate based on their skill set?

○ Yes
○ No

If so, what web service(s) did you use
[   ]

What do you recommend as ways to build expertise with a skill?

	Effectiveness
Read a Book (paper or online)	[▾]
Take on a Project at Work	[▾]
Take a Class	[▾]
Volunteer	[▾]
Join an Organization	[▾]

Other (please specify)
[   ]

Do you think a skill set is an effective way to summarize a professional background?

Not Effective		Somewhat Effective		Very Effective
○	○	○	○	○

Other (please specify)
[   ]

Appendix: Resources

Planning Stage

- Planning To Learn Skills

    - **Gallup Strengths Planner** (www.gallupstrengthscenter.com) provides a well-conceived strengths assessment service, which identifies core-competencies and how to leverage and develop them.

    - **MyPlan.com** (www.myplan.com) provides personality, interests, and skills tests and other resources to make you self-aware.

    - **Kuder** (www.kuder.com) provides various career assessment tools for all stages in a career – middle school up to early career professionals.

- Ways To Learn Skills

    - There are thousands of colleges or universities where you can earn associates, bachelors, or masters' degrees. Some online resources that can help you decide on a college include: **Princeton Review** (www.princetonreview.com) and **US News** (www.usnews.com/education).

    - There are many ways to learn particular technologies or software languages, search on them to find online classes, videos, forums, or books.

        - **YouTube** (www.youtube.com) has video tutorials.

        - **Amazon** (www.amazon.com) offers books that have been ranked and reviewed.

        - **Pluralsight** (www.pluralsight.com) offers a wide array of technical classes.

        - Go to the website of the company that is leading the technology. For example, visit **Microsoft** (www.microsoft.com/net) if you want to learn to develop websites with ASP .Net.

    - **SkillSoft** (www.skillsoft.com) offers a service where employers invest in online training to improve their employees' performance.

    - **Free Online Courses (MOOCs)** are a popular way to learn skills – several million people have signed for classes since they were introduced two years ago. Some of the classes provide certifications upon completing the class, and some organizations are advocating actual college credits.

- **Coursera** (www.coursera.org)
- **EdX** (www.edx.org)
- **Udacity** (www.udacity.com)

o **Enstitute** (www.enstituteu.com) offers apprenticeships for careers in high-growth industries.

Building Stage

o **Skills Based Approach** (www.skillsbasedapproach.com) provides templates where you keep track of your progress in learning and building an expertise with skills.

o Learn from a supervisor or professor about your performance and continue being assertive regarding advancing the development of skills.

Presenting Stage

o **LinkedIn** (www.linkedin.com) is a professional social media service. You should maintain a skill set on their platform for two reasons. First, they built a powerful search platform *Recruiter* where recruiters target skill sets. Second, they have an interface where connections endorse a level of expertise with skills.

o **MonsterJobs** (www.monster.com) is an online job board. They built a search platform called *Power Resume* where recruiters search on skill sets to retrieve a ranked list of candidates. So if you are actively or passively seeking employment, you should maintain a skill set with this service.

o **TheProfessionalWebsite** (www.theprofessionalwebsite.com) provides a personal website service and skills sets are tightly interwoven into the interface.

o **SkillsPages** (www.skillpages.com) is a search engine based on skill sets. You publish a skill set to a profile and interested parties (such as recruiters, potential employers, and consultants) search on skill sets to match their needs.

Validation Stage

- Finding Ways to Validate

    - Most professions have an umbrella organization that represents them, and they usually provide information about certifications. For example, accountants can find information from **American Institute of CPAs** (www.aicpa.org).

    - **CareerOneStop** (www.careerinfonet.org/certifications_new) provides a search engine where you can find certifications. They are sponsored by the US Department of Labor.

    - Similar to learning from a company that provides the technology, you can usually become certified. For example, **Cisco** (www.cisco.com/web/learning/certifications) provides various certifications for using their network hardware and software.

- Presenting Your Validations

    - **TheProfessionalWebsite** (www.theprofessionalwebite.com) has an interface where you present all possible ways to validate your skills.

    - **LinkedIn** (www.linkedin.com) allows for you to be endorsed by connections, and with the network effect, this becomes a powerful way validate skills.

    - **Wordpress** (www.wordpress.com), **Blogger** (www.blogger.com) and **Tumblr** (www.tumblr.com) are blogging platforms you can use to establish credibility with your skill set by sharing insights and knowledge.

    - **Mozilla Online Badges** (openbadges.org) is still work in progress but will be a popular, powerful way to validate skills and achievements.

(Endnotes)

1. "Future Work Skills 2020," *Institute for the Future for University of Phoenix Research Institute*, 2011, http://www.scribd.com/doc/94872255.
2. Definition of terms, http://en.wikipedia.org/wiki/Soft_skills
3. Travis Bradberry, and Jean Greaves, "Emotional Intelligence 2.0," (San Diego: TalentSmart, 2009), pp. 21.
4. George Anders, "How LinkedIn Has Turned Your Resume into a Cash Machine," *Forbes*, June 27, 2012, http://www.forbes.com/sites/georgeanders/2012/06/27/how-linkedin-strategy.
5. 2011 Annual Report for MonsterJobs.
6. Carl Bialik, "Seven Careers in a Lifetime? Think Twice, Researchers Say," *Wall Street Journal*, September 4, 2010, http://online.wsj.com/article/SB10001424052748704206804575468162805877990.html.
7. Peter Rusev, "One Billion Endorsements Given on LinkedIn," *LinkedIn*, March 6, 2013, http://blog.linkedin.com/2013/03/06/1-billion-endorsements-given-on-linkedin-infographic.
8. "Summary: Skills Based Approach," *TheProfessionalWebsite*, 2012, http://www.scribd.com/doc/117176551.
9. Seth Godin, *Icarus Deception: How High Will You Fly?* (New York: Penguin, 2012).
10. Gretchen Spreitzer and Christine Porath, "Creating Sustainable Performance," *Harvard Business Review*, January 2012, http://hbr.org/2012/01/creating-sustainable-performance.
11. Cal Newport, *So Good They Can't Ignore You: Why Skills Trump Passion in the Quest for Work You Love* (New York: Hachett, 2012).
12. Seth Godin, *Linchpin: Are You Indispensable?* (New York: Penguin, 2010).
13. Larry Bird, *Drive: The Story of My Life* (New York: Bantam, 1990).
14. http://astronauts.nasa.gov/default.htm
15. Po Bronson, and Ashley Merryman, *Top Dog: The Science of Winning and Losing* (New York: Hachette, 2013, pp. 162).
16. Kelsey Sheehy, "Ten Medical Schools with the Lowest Acceptance Rates," *US News*, August 14, 2012, http://www.usnews.com/education/best-graduate-schools/the-short-list-grad-school/articles/2012/08/14/10-medical-schools-with-the-lowest-acceptance-rates.
17. Dorie Clark, *Reinventing You* (Boston, MA: Harvard Business Review Press, 2013).
18. Karen Kang, *Branding Pays: The Five-Step System to Reinvent Your Personal Brand* (Palo Alto, CA: Branding Pays LLC, 2013).
19. Dan Schawbel, *Me 2.0: Build a Powerful Brand to Achieve Career Success* (New York: Kaplan Publishing, 2009).
20. IBM ad in Wired magazine, issue 21.01.
21. Leonard Schlesinger, Charles Kiefer, and Paul Brown, "Career Plans Are Dangerous," *Harvard Business Review*, March 2012, http://blogs.hbr.org/cs/2012/03/career_plans_are_dangerous.html.
22. Clayton Christensen, "How Will You Measure Your Life," *Harvard Business Review*, July 2010, http://hbr.org/2010/07/how-will-you-measure-your-life/ar/1.
23. http://www.ibankingfaq.com/category/banking-lifestyle.
24. Amy Gallo, "How to Master a New Skill," *Harvard Business Review*, November 2012, http://blogs.hbr.org/hmu/2012/11/how-to-master-a-new-skill.html.
25. "A Pulse on Talent Management in the Year Ahead," Right Management: ManpowerGroup, 2012, pp 10.
26. Brian Hernandez, "84% of Workers Want to Quit Jobs, Find New Gigs in 2011," *Business News Daily*, December 2010, http://www.businessnewsdaily.com/536-84-percent-employees-seek-new-jobs-2011.html.
27. Sean Conrad, "Find Organizations that Support Career Development," *Simply Hired*, December 2012, http://blog.simplyhired.com/2012/12/find-organizations-that-support-your-career-development.html.
28. Kevin Carey, "Show Me Your Badge," *The New York Times*, November 12, 2012, http://www.nytimes.com/2012/11/04/education/edlife/show-me-your-badge.html?pagewanted=all&_r=0.
29. Peter Sterlacci, "Personal Brands Are Like a Sweet Onion," *Personal Branding Blog*, January 2013, http://www.personalbrandingblog.com/personal-brands-are-like-a-sweet-onion.
30. Schawbel, *Me 2.0*, pp.2.
31. Douglas Belkin, and Melissa Korn, "Colleges' Latest Offer: Deals," *Wall Street Journal*, March 12, 2013.
32. Ben Casselman, "College Grads May Be Stuck in Low-Skill Jobs," *Wall Street Journal*, March 26, 2013.
33. Hansen, Randall Dr; Hansen, Katherine Dr. "What Do Employers Really Want? Top Skills and Values Employers Seek from Job-Seekers." Quintessential Careers, http://www.quintcareers.com/job_skills_values.html
34. Institute for the Future, "Future Work Skills 2020."
35. Bradberry and Greaves, *Emotional Intelligence 2.0*.
36. "Open Badges Working Papers", https://wiki.mozilla.org/File:OpenBadges-Working-Paper_012312.pdf

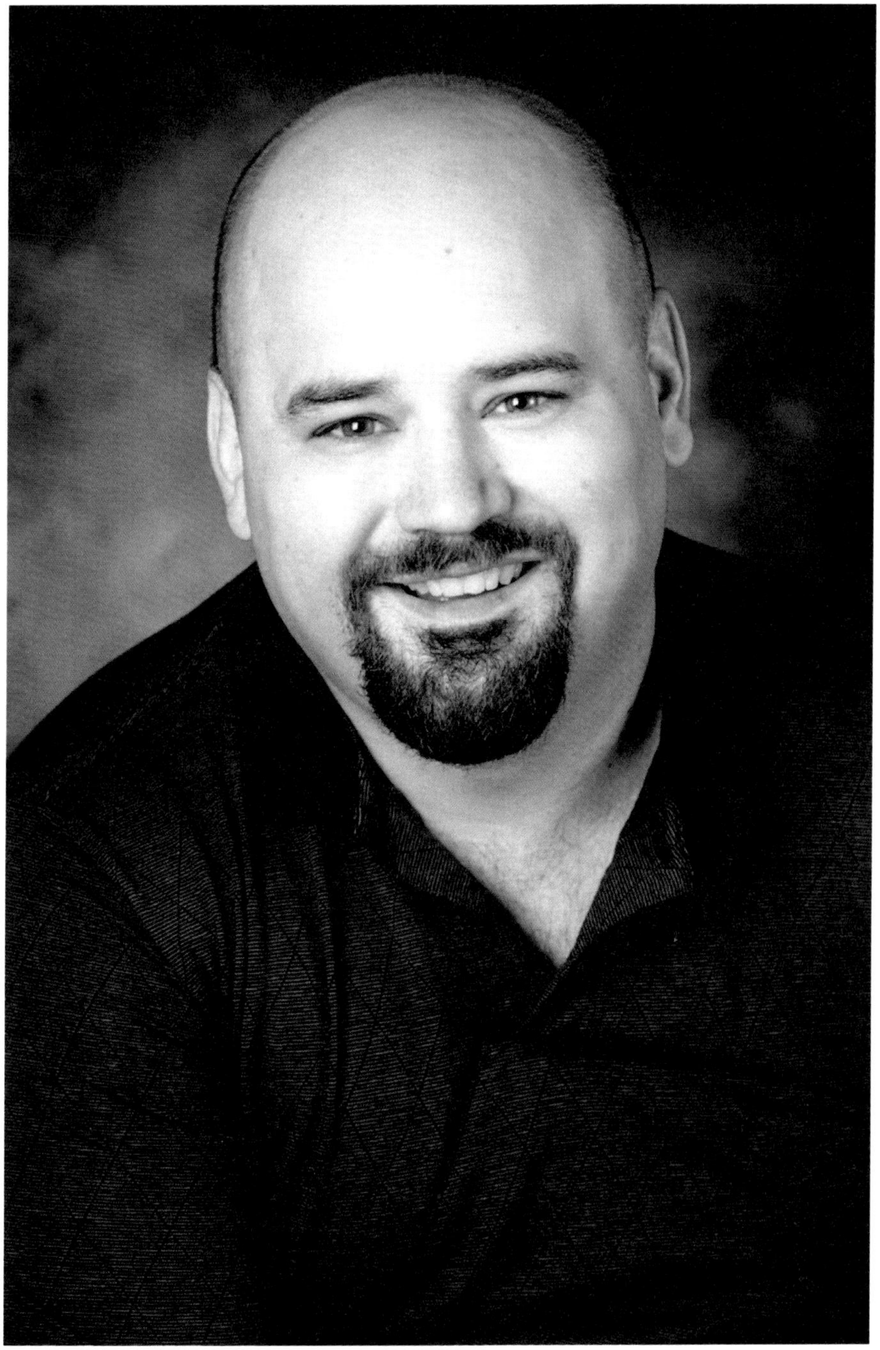

Edwards Brothers Malloy
Oxnard, CA USA
August 5, 2013